The Young Inheritors

THE YOUNG INHERITORS

A Portrait of Israel's Children

by

YEHUDA AVNER

Photographs by

GEMMA LEVINE

With an introduction by Herman Wouk

THE DIAL PRESS

New York

Published by
The Dial Press
1 Dag Hammarskjold Plaza
New York, New York 10017

The works of art that appear in photographs in this book are:

The Silent Cry by Leah Michaelson, p. 32.
Dry Bones, pp. 36–37.
The Ghetto Uprising by Nathan Rapoport, pp. 42–43, 45.
Sculpture by Tamarkin, p. 48.
The Last March by Nathan Rapoport, p. 51.

Text copyright © 1982 by Yehuda Avner
Photographs copyright © 1982 by Gemma Levine
Introduction copyright © 1982 by Herman Wouk

Manufactured in the United States of America
First printing
Design by Francesca Belanger

Library of Congress Cataloging in Publication Data

Avner, Yehuda.
The young inheritors.

1. Youth—Israel.   2. Israel—Social conditions.
I. Levine, Gemma.   II. Title.
HQ799.17A9   305.2'3'095694   81-9799
ISBN 0-385-27222-7   AACR2

To Shai and Tanya

Contents

Introduction

Of making books about Israel—that forty-mile-wide sliver of land on the eastern Mediterranean shore which commands more of the world's headlines than countries a thousand times as large in area and population—there is no end. Here is a book that was worth doing and is worth reading.

Too many of the books are about the Israel of the headlines. That land is a media phantom. There is no such place. It is an abstract brewed by reporters, commentators, best-seller writers, sociologists, political scientists, television interviewers, and the ranters in the UN. The geographical Israel, the green pleasant vibrant land I know, bears little resemblance to that chimera.

There are, to be sure, good serious books about Israel. The Middle East is today at the fulcrum of world affairs, and Israel is in a sense at the fulcrum of the Middle East. So a blaze of inquiring intelligence beats on this tiny country of three million and each year brings substantial new academic works on aspects of the Jewish state. But such works are not for the general audience.

Yehuda Avner, the author of this book, is an Israeli civil servant of British origin. He knows Israel as a fighting man, a paterfamilias, a public servant, and a longtime confidant of the nation's leaders; and he here presents his homeland from the viewpoint of the young people.

It is a useful perspective. These Young Inheritors, after all, have the greatest stake in the land. They are its defenders, its future, and in large measure its present. What they feel and think and say about Israel, the things they do, the way they look while doing them, all suggest what Israel is truly like. These young people are there on the ground, under the Israeli sky, in Israel's wind, snow, and rain, as well as in the famous dazzling sunshine. Theirs is not the Israel seen from posh hotel windows or in quick television once-overs. Gemma Levine's revealing photographs complement a profuse array of anecdotes and quotations, for by and large, Mr. Avner has sensibly allowed the Young Inheritors to speak for themselves.

Nothing is scamped. The conflict with the Arabs is faced head-on. So is the problem of the underprivileged "eastern community," the Sephardic Jews; those youngsters state plainly their caustic cynical views of the country which for a long time mishandled their immigrant parents and themselves. We meet the kibbutz youngsters, coolly weighing the pros and cons of their communal way of life. We encounter the nation's swirl of religious differences and tensions. Mr. Avner even gives us an amusing rundown on the meanings of the subtle variations in the skullcaps worn by the faithful.

The candid chapter on the ambivalence of the Young Inheritors toward the holocaust is quite striking. These young people are not mourners or moaners over the tragic Jewish past. They are the heart of its lively present, and they are not very patient with ancestral memories. Mr. Avner clearly thinks that they have been too much cut off from their past. But if they are now seeking out in some tentative degree their sources—their sacred literature, and their three-millennia history—their backs are certainly turned to the past of the ghetto, the shtetl, the exile, and the Wandering Jew. They are home. Deeply though they loathe war and love peace, they love Israel above all. These are not warlike young people, just toughened realists who will fight hard if they must for their land.

So here is a refreshing picture of the Jewish state, seen through the unsparing eyes of the young people who are resolved to establish it in peace; and who, on the evidence of their deeds, their words, and their faces pictured in these pages, can do it. I know these Young Inheritors, and in this book they appear before you as they are.

28 December 1980   *Herman Wouk*

The Young Inheritors

Prologue:

The Child in El Arish

In the early hours of a Sunday morning in May 1979, two tourist buses, one Egyptian, the other Israeli, wound their separate ways along the coastal road of northern Sinai bound for El Arish, a sand-swept Arab town anchored in desert dunes. The passengers were scarred men, some lame, some paralyzed, some disfigured. Many wore uniforms adorned with battle ribbons. Their only baggage was crutches, wheelchairs, and walking canes.

The travelers had traversed this terrain before. They had once moved toward each other across the Sinai Peninsula as whole men, in tanks, in half-tracks, in gun carriers, and in armored command cars. Their aim had been to kill; failing that, they had maimed one another for life. Now, these men, disabled veterans of the wars between Egypt and Israel, were closing in on each other again. President Sadat of Egypt and Prime Minister Begin of Israel were bringing them together to meet, to shake hands, and to vow to each other: No more war! The peace treaty between the two countries, signed earlier that year in Washington, was to be symbolically celebrated at El Arish in a unique rendezvous of chivalry and reconciliation.

The Egyptian bus was the first to arrive. Haltingly, the passengers alighted and walked, limped, and wheeled themselves into the shady interior of a flag-bedecked recreation hall. Soon, the Israeli bus drew up and, with crutches, canes, and wheelchairs, the invalids shuffled their way inside.

As they entered, the scene froze. Egyptian and Israeli eyes momentarily locked in what seemed a suspense of conflicting emotion.

Israeli graffiti: The children have experienced at least one war or the threat of war every decade.

A blind man escorted by a child stepped forward from the Israeli group. Even as he moved, a legless Egyptian officer wheeled his chair toward him and, with no words spoken, the two veterans shook hands.

At that instant a deafening cheer of approval resounded throughout the crowded hall. Lines melted in a boisterous huddle of embraces, handshakes, and hefty backslaps. With laughter and tears the wounded men of the War of Independence of 1948, the Sinai war of 1956, the Six Day War of 1967, the war of attrition of 1969–1970, and the Yom Kippur War of 1973, greeted each other with cries of *"Shalom!" "Salaam!"* "Peace!"

4

Enveloped in the midst of this raucous camaraderie, the child in El Arish clung tightly to his blind father. He appeared bewildered, frightened even, his eyes darting back and forth at the animated faces of Arab and Jew. For nothing in his young experience had prepared him for this. From the day he could talk and walk he had played escort to a father who would never see because he had been made blind by Arabs. They had always been the enemy and, by definition, they were bad.

Sensing his son's apprehension, the blind man took the youngster into his embrace. "Don't be afraid," he said. "These Arabs are good."

I

Children
of the
Conflict

Gilli, Aged Fifteen, the Old City, Jerusalem

When I was small, about nine or ten, I remember thinking to myself that there were two kinds of Arabs—good ones and bad. The good ones were those who came to my dad's shop, or to our house on some job, or the owner of the kiosk—Massoud—near Jaffa Gate who always gave me a candy with the lollipop I bought on my way home from school. The bad ones were those who hid bombs in places or who threw stones—things like that. Now that I'm older and have grown up here in the Old City with Arabs all around, I can tell you that some are bad and some are good and there are lots of others in between. I suppose it's the same the world over, people I mean. We take living with the Arabs so much for granted. We've lived with them and the conflict all our lives. Most of us most of the time don't think about it particularly—not as a problem—unless something terrible happens like a war or a bad terrorist attack. We're so used to it— hearing on TV what the Arabs say and what we say, and the fact that we all know that when school's over we'll go into the army. I certainly don't hate Arabs; I don't think kids do. Wait a minute, that's not true. There's this boy in our youth movement—he's a year older than me—who can't stand them. His brother was killed in southern Lebanon when we attacked the PLO. I don't know what, but it did something to him. He says all he's waiting for is to get into the army. I think he's looking for revenge. But most of us, we don't hate and we don't love. I guess we're wary on occasion. All we want is to get along with them in peace—like we're supposed to be doing now with the Egyptians. You know, the peace treaty and all that. We talk about that together sometimes, me and my friends, how long it's going to last. My father's been in three wars and I'd rather not have another when I'm older, in the army. In Hebrew we have an expression: Kabdeihu v'chashdeihu—it means, respect and suspect. I guess that's as good a way as any of saying it. I respect them, sure, but so long as things are as they are I also suspect.

"Children of the shelters" . . .

For as long as anyone can remember, the Jewish state has been in conflict with Arabs and the imprint of this conflict is etched deep into the national psyche. Israel's youngsters have experienced at least one war every decade. Ask parents about their own childhood and many will recite memories of school alerts, emergency mobilizations, air raid sirens, and anxious mothers hurrying children into basements and bomb shelters.

Looking back, one counts years in which warfare and the threat of it were so repetitive that the average schoolboy approaching the age of eighteen—the age of the compulsory draft—would, with understandable uneasiness, take it for granted that sooner than later he would have to fight. The older the high school in Israel, the longer the roll of honor on its wall—homage to the lads of the class of '45 who fell in the war of '48; the class of '48 in the war of '56; the class of '56 in the war of '67; the class of '67 in the war of '69–'70; the classes of '69 and '70 in the war of '73; and the dates and names inscribed in between and beyond, reminders of frontier campaigns, border raids, and terrorist attacks. Not until the mid-seventies did Israel experience a year in which it did not bury some young soldier killed on some field of battle.

on the oft-troubled Lebanese border.

Were Israel that much larger and its population bigger, the sacrifices might have been less fiercely personalized. But the country is little (about forty miles at the widest) and the nation small (hardly more than three million). Most families know some family who has lost someone. Until the peace treaty with Egypt, the only boundary not subject to armed siege was the sea.

No wonder, then, that the intimacy of the struggle always counted for much. With geographic margins so narrow, the people—the sea at their backs—so tightly compacted together, and the enemy round about so numerous, every new war was perceived to be a struggle for national survival. Nothing has galvanized this nation of disparate communities more than the sense of common Jewish fate, the folk-feeling that in defending the land its people were literally protecting their homes, their families, and above all, the children,

בור בטחון
EMERGENCY
SHELTER

A sign as old as the country.

from yet another holocaust of Jews. To understand this is to capture something of the passion and the pathos of this very old-new nation.

There was little one could ever do to insulate the youngsters from the atmosphere of threat whenever it came. Everything they saw and heard—the mobilization of fathers and brothers, the radio, newspaper and television headlines, the buses commandeered to transport

"Security pits" are dug in the vicinity of public buildings— a sandbagged hole in which to toss a suspicious-looking object.

חב"ת בטחון

soldiers to the front, the antiblast tape on the windows, the posters appealing for blood donors, the hasty blackout precautions—everything, everywhere announced to them that they were sharing a great emergency. And always, their collective response was one of a deep sense of belonging, of intense involvement. In towns and villages youngsters big and little would organize themselves, performing acts of voluntary service with an enterprise that left worrying mothers amazed and tremendously proud. Obviously there was fear; it was as if the boys and girls were trying to suppress and drown their anxieties in a mass outpouring of physical energies: digging trenches, filling sandbags, sorting mail, delivering messages, learning first aid—anything that might keep them busy.

Mercifully, the fighting, though never far from the children, hardly engulfed them. In the wake of the War of Independence in 1948, a military doctrine of sorts was elaborated that was to rescue most from the bodily horrors of the battles yet to rage. Its point of reference was the premise that Israel had no strategic defensive depth. In the north the heights of Syria and Lebanon looked down

Public shelters often double as recreation halls.

Gadna (the Youth Corps) caters to high school students, offering summer camps, pre-army drills, courses in good citizenship, and a variety of volunteer civic pursuits. (*left*) A lesson in self-defense . . .

upon the villages of Galilee. In the south the port of Eilat was sandwiched tight between Jordan and Egypt, and the Egyptian-controlled Gaza district protruded arrow-deep into the southern heartland. In the center the mountains of Judea and Samaria, then occupied by Jordan, towered above the narrow coastal strip eight to fifteen miles wide, that strip in which two thirds of Israel lives. Jerusalem was a divided city, pockmarked with trenches, barbed wire, and mine fields, and sliced by high concrete walls with a litter-strewn no-man's-land in between.

in communications . . .

This was the map in 1967 before the Six Day War. Most Israeli homes were in range of enemy artillery and, frequently, of machine-gun fire. Youngsters on hikes were conditioned to keep a lookout for signposts which seemed to pepper the length of the land: Danger. Frontier Ahead!

Hence, the strategic thinking which postulated that Israel must never be caught off guard, and that it dare not grant the military initiative to the other side. To do so could mean carnage, even extinction, for the only retreat was into the sea. When, as in 1956 and 1967, the nation faced dire threat, it was compelled to mobilize rapidly and strike hard, before the enemy blow fell, so as to carry the front away—as far as possible away—from the centers of population.

Once, on Yom Kippur day, 1973, Israel was taken by surprise. Its forces initially reeled back before massive Egyptian and Syrian

and in marksmanship.

(*Overleaf*) At play in the Old City, Jerusalem: Children see nothing ominous in the anti-terrorist precautions on which they are reared; they take them for granted.

invasions. The price in blood of this most terrible of all the wars was agonizing. But Israel proper and its civilians were again saved, for by this time, between them and the invading forces stood the defensive depth of the Sinai desert and the Golan Heights and the mountains of Judea and Samaria, gained six years earlier in the Six Day War.

The country, then, though repeatedly and ferociously war-tried, was never geographically war-torn and its children, though knowing of war, were always largely spared the ravages of warfare. With the exception of frontier areas, the scenes of battle never engulfed their homes. Thus, in the case of most, daily life has generally been much more prosaic than many a dramatized image of it would suggest—the image of children growing up Spartanlike, in a society living perilously by its wits and by the sword, embattled, beleaguered, and besieged. At times Israel was like that, with security and survival seemingly hanging by a thread, and the challenge of defense remains awesomely acute still. Some historians writing their chapters about the battles and the blockades will no doubt be tempted to describe the Jewish state's first decades as the desperate years of defiant defense. But to the mass of the people the overview is somewhat different. Their perceptions and preoccupations, and certainly those of their children, are dominated not by the wars—though their sacrifice is never forgotten—but by the domestic pursuits of living in between them. If their daily tale is not a tranquil one, it is, given the unique Israeli condition, normal enough. To the children, it would seem to be entirely so.

Childhood in Israel is what healthy childhood anywhere should mean: play and school and chores and make-believe and mischief and as jolly a time as might be had. The children grow up as children are wont to do, experimenting and discovering and learning the good things of life and adjusting to the background noises of those nasty, ugly things they wish would go away but won't, like the road accidents and bathers drowning and planes crashing and people's homes burning. The cacophony that distantly intrudes upon the world of every child is augmented in the case of the Israeli youngster by one further ugly sound which won't go away—the trouble with the Arabs. Born as he or she is into it, the child lives with it, is aware and is wary of it, and accepts it for what it is—an unpleasant fact of life, part of the scheme of things.

Thus, just as there may be a time to learn in school from the traffic policeman the elements of road safety, so there is a time to learn from the police sapper the rudiments of precaution against ter-

(*Opposite*) Though the country has been repeatedly war-tried, its children have largely been spared the ravages of warfare.

16

rorist violence. And just as the one will impress upon the children to look both ways before crossing the road, so will the other emphasize the need to keep a sharp eye open for suspicious-looking objects, such as an unattended shopping bag in the market place or a parcel left on the bus. As it is important always to be reminded that alertness can save lives, a poster is on permanent display in the school corridor or classroom depicting and describing the tricks of the terrorist trade. It will carry the bold-letter advice to touch nothing and to inform the police of everything that might not be what it appears to be. In 1974 in an Upper Galilee school, children were taken hostage and sixteen of them were mowed down by the terrorists. Subsequently, a variety of innocent-looking objects, deadly to the touch

but which children would naturally want to pick up—like ball-point pens booby-trapped and packed with dynamite—were found in a number of school yards. Nothing quite as diabolic as this had happened before and the conclusion was drawn: Schools and playgrounds had become chosen targets for terrorist murder. Police, parents, and educational authorities got together and the results of their action may be seen today in the vicinity of every school in Israel. By law, during school hours a parent or senior pupil stands duty in each school yard to make sure that there are no hidden explosive devices around and no suspicious-looking characters lurking about who might turn out to be Palestine Liberation Organization terrorists.

Israel's streets and parks are carefree places and are usually safer to tread than those of many a metropolis elsewhere.

Occasionally, a loud blast does go off somewhere, and when this happens, youngsters within earshot have learned to keep a discerning ear open for one of two follow-up sounds. If they hear the noise of aircraft, they know the bang was a sonic boom from the jet-patrolled skies above. If ambulance and police sirens sound, they assume it was a bomb. Then, the sensible ones make a call home or to the nearest neighbor with a telephone, just to check in. At such moments parents want to know where exactly their children are. Thankfully, most loud blasts are sonic booms.

To the youngsters this reality is far less ominous or grim than the description of it sounds. The caution on which they are reared and the precautions with which they are surrounded are as natural and as familiar to them as the traffic light on the street corner or the fire extinguisher on the school wall or the father's khaki kit-bag in the closet at home, packed and ready in case of a reserve summons. Indeed, lest it be deduced that an atmosphere of permanent brooding violence stalks the children as they go about their outdoor pursuits, let it here be recorded: Israel's city streets and parks are generally carefree places in which youngsters roam and in which they play after as well as before dark. The places are, in truth, far safer to tread than many an urban thoroughfare and park in many a metropolis elsewhere. Israel has some problems, but parental anxiety over the nocturnal survival-factor of their children outdoors is not one of them.

There is one corner of Israel—the far north of Galilee—where it is not quite like that; where children live close to a live battlefront and within range of its intermittent convulsions. These are the youngsters whose homes are the mountain kibbutz and moshav (cooperative) villages adjacent to the volatile Lebanese frontier and who live in the towns of Kiryat Shemona and Nahariya not far behind. For them the Arab-Israeli conflict is not a distant cacophony; it is a reality inducing that sixth-sense instinctive alertness imbibed only by those long accustomed to life within earshot of war. In these villages and towns children have long since learned to identify the whistle of Katyusha rockets, to play not too far from shelters, to treat with respect emergency exercises in classrooms, to inform parents of their whereabouts, and to live with the sight of armed soldiers and their armored vehicles.

For years the Lebanese frontier was the most tranquil of them all, until the early 1970s. Then, the PLO moved in from Jordan, deploying its major bases inside Lebanese territory, focusing on Israel's border zone. What ensued was unspeakable tragedy. Lebanon, a

(*Opposite*) Children take it for granted that their fathers have to spend about a month a year on active service. Israel's army is composed mainly of its civilian reserve.

country once known as the Switzerland of the Middle East, was plunged into internecine warfare that within a few years reduced it to a bleeding, mutilated body of a state, its battles raging and ranging among Lebanese Christians and Christians and Moslems and Syrians and PLO. The shadow of that terrible violence has stretched across Israel's northern frontier. It is a war contained next door but which sometimes comes crashing across into Israeli homes through bombardment and, when the terrorists can, atrocity. The children of this little corner of Israel live with these recurrent tensions just as the "shelter children" of the Jordan valley had once lived with theirs.

The "shelter children" were the youngsters of the late sixties in the kibbutz and moshav villages along the Jordanian frontier. It was a bad time for them. A static war of attrition was ranging along the length of the River Jordan, again spearheaded by the PLO. The shelling of the villages was so incessant, so intense that for months the village children literally slept, ate, played, and attended classes underground. The simple solution would have been to evacuate them to the rear, but this the parents refused to do. Their decision to keep the children with them was not irrational patriotic zeal; it was psychological common sense. Even as the war of attrition escalated, they deliberated long and hard with psychologists, child psychiatrists, security experts, and most of all, with themselves, about what to do.

The youngsters are their own traffic wardens and the older ones patrol their own school yards.

(*Opposite*) In times of tension, children living in the vicinity of a troubled frontier tend to play in the shadows of their shelters.

22

Assembly at a Gadna camp.

Their conclusion was that to separate the children from parents and homes would induce greater long-term trauma than letting them be in the shelters underground. Moreover, their evacuation would so undermine morale as to spell the possible collapse of the village community network along the whole valley. If the shelling and incursions made normal life difficult, the departure of the children would make it impossible.

Anybody who visited these villages during that attrition war heard about the psychological stress of the "children of the shelters." But time was to vindicate the decision to let them stay put. Whatever traumas the youngsters suffered proved to be far more transient than those of youngsters who had been evacuated in war elsewhere. Years later the example of these parents and children was to be emulated by those on the Lebanese frontier, though mercifully, these villages have never been put to quite the same exacting test.

Though elsewhere throughout the country many children may tend to accept the ongoing conflict with the Arabs as some kind of distracting aberration, their feelings toward Arabs as individuals are often more emotionally charged. Communication is invariably circumspect. The children are too used to hearing the word Arab in a context of threat not to be wary of its stereotyped image. The older the boys and girls are, the closer they come to that inevitable day of the draft, knowing that the enemy they face will be Arab.

Before the 1967 Six Day War most youngsters had few occasions to meet Arabs and those whom they did see were citizens of Israel.

In those days Israel's total Arab population, Moslem and Christian, numbered hardly four hundred thousand. Some towns, notably Jaffa, Haifa, and Acre, had Arab communities, but the majority lived in their traditional rural settings in Galilee up north or in the Negev desert bedouin encampments down south. Relations were generally peaceful and political unrest was uncommon. When city kids journeyed through these areas, on school outings or youth movement hikes, the encounters were habitually hospitable and always exotic.

Then came June 5, 1967. Arab armies stood poised along every frontier and the Israelis, outnumbered and outgunned, felt surrounded, abandoned, and imperiled. In a desperate drive their forces struck out, and six days later it was all over. On the heels of the stunning victory came relief, respite, and the Palestinian Arabs. Less than a week before, they had been the enemy on the other side of the fortified armistice line awaiting Arab victory. Now, as the dust settled, these more than one million Palestinian Arabs made their uneasy rendezvous with the Jewish state and the Jewish state with them. Down came the fortifications along the line that snaked through the length of the land between the Jordan River and the Mediterranean Sea. Down came the barriers across divided Jerusalem with its 85,000 Arabs, across Judea and Samaria (the West Bank) with its 700,000 Arabs, and across the Gaza Strip with its 400,000 Arabs.

With the removal of the barbed wire fences and the defenses, the Palestinian Arabs crossed freely into Israel, back and forth, to shop, to trade, to work, to study, to enjoy the beaches, and in some cases to try to plant bombs. Overnight, Israel's city youngsters began seeing Arabs in numbers and in places they had rarely been before.

Now on a normal working day as many as one hundred thousand Palestinian Arabs might cross into Israel proper on jobs of one sort or another. Their conspicuousness is enough to tint the complexion of the Jewish state's demography. In parts of the country children see them everywhere, on building sites, on farms, in factories, garages, workshops, and sometimes in their own homes working as craftsmen, house painters, or janitors. The overall panorama of this daily human interaction is generally peaceful and pragmatic. But then a bomb explodes somewhere—a brutal reminder that over it all hovers the dispute. The undercover emissary of violence, as every child quickly learns, remains the PLO, whose target is always exclusively civilian, be it a bomb in a bag in a bus station or a booby trap or a rocket lobbed across the border. Though such incidents are infrequent and do not interrupt the normal flow of life, they are enough

to make youngsters mindful that not every Arab they see in the street is a friend and that, given the chance, some might even be killers. Hence the wariness.

The more the cycle and circle of human contact between Arabs and Jews interlock, the more equivocal does this generalization become. There are thousands of Israeli children in different spots around the country who have virtually been brought up among Arabs since 1967. A good many of them go about unperturbed, doing their own thing in surroundings that are Arab. Take Yossi, for example, a thirteen-year old from Kiryat Arba, Hebron's Jewish suburb. Asked whether the Hebronites make him feel uneasy, he shrugs the question off. He was just about born when the suburb was founded and the sights, sounds, and people of Hebron are all that he has ever known. To him they are the natural backdrop to his domestic scene. Yossi says he has no compunctions about buying in the Arab market, traveling on an Arab bus, or even occasionally kicking a ball around with an Arab youngster. Yossi and most of his friends already have a working knowledge of Arabic. His father, a onetime American, contends that for all the political tremors, and even the incidents of violence, the daily relationship between the people of Hebron and Kiryat Arba is not much different from that prevailing between certain ethnic communities in the United States. In both instances it is intelligent not to roam everywhere unarmed, he says.

Children living in the recently established Jewish rural settlements that have sprouted up here and there in the contested hills of Judea and Samaria seem to display no particular complexes as they go about their wanderings. Relations with the scattered Arab villages are generally correct, at times even cordial, and one sees many a youngster blithely occupied with his or her own pursuits while Arab farmers carry on their labors in fields nearby. Nonetheless, with nightfall the settlements mount guard.

Shula, a freckle-faced, ginger-headed sixteen-year old from one such settlement, Karnei Shomron, describes things this way: "We don't play with their kids and they don't play with us but we get along from afar. They have their ways and we have ours." And what of the conflict and the controversy over these new settlements? Shula's answer is: "Sometimes, one of theirs may throw a stone at a passing car, but we learn to live with it. We belong here as much as they do. Once, a few of us were on a hike to find an archaeological dig we'd heard about. We went walking and walking until we realized we were lost. So we asked an Arab boy—he was about our age—

working in a field close by for the direction. He said he'd show us the way and he did. He was so nice about it I asked him his name. Jihad, he said. We thought we hadn't heard right but that's what he said, Jihad. *Jihad* is Arabic for 'holy war.' That put my back up, so I said to him, 'You'd better do something about that name of yours because we're going to be here together forever. This may be Palestine to you,' I said, 'but to us it's Eretz Israel. Read your Bible,' I said. Do you know what he did? He just gave us a smile and ran off. To think a parent would give a name like that, Jihad! He seemed such a nice kid, but that's how it is, I guess.''

Nathanya is Israel's most popular seaside resort. Less than ten miles away is an Arab town called Tulkarm, which before 1967 was on the other side of the armistice divide. David, sixteen, lives in Nathanya. He is a lanky lad with spectacles that give him a rather studious look, and he has two big passions—building things and playing chess. His father owns an auto-repair shop by the Tel Aviv–Haifa highway where the road branches off near Nathanya. Three Tulkarmites work for him, two mechanics and an electrician. They know David well because he is always visiting the shop building his gadgets. Mussa, the Arab electrician, has a sixteen-year-old boy called Dawood, which is David in Arabic. Once, David went with his father to Mussa's home and the boys met. David recalls the encounter: "We just stared at each other and said nothing for about a quarter of an hour while our fathers talked business. I wanted to get out quickly. I felt uncomfortable. But then I spied this chess set lying on a shelf. It was a beauty, one of those ornamental ones, and I went over to examine it. Dawood got up, brought it down, and gestured he was ready to take me on. He beat me in six moves. From then on we've been playing fairly regularly and now that I know some Arabic

While Jerusalem sleeps, a father-and-son team, members of the volunteer Civil Defense Guard, patrol the streets.

and he some Hebrew, we've become kind of friends. We talk about football and movies and things like that, but we never talk politics. Once we did and we nearly had a fight—after the bus was shot up by the PLO at the country club. Dawood thinks Arafat is a hero and I tell him he's a cold-blooded killer. For weeks after that I didn't see Dawood, but then we got back together again and we're still playing

chess. The strange thing is I'll be going into the army in a couple of years and I hope, for both our sakes, I won't have to fight him. I'd rather lose to Dawood in chess than win him in a war. When you come to think about it, our chess playing is a kind of a private war. Every win is a victory. The day I play him a normal game, I'll know we have peace.''

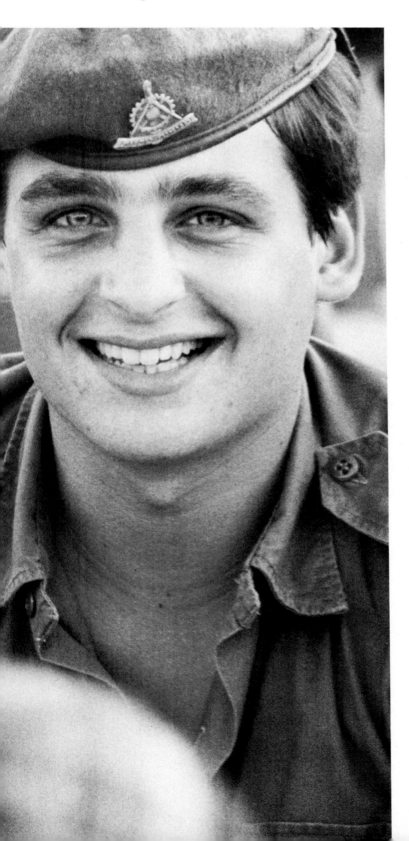

They tend to scoff at their own patriotism and laugh at their own fears.

II

"Masada Shall Not Fall Again"

Ovad, Aged Eleven, Ramat Hasharon, Tel Aviv

My mother has a number stamped on her arm, her left arm. It's printed in light blue ink. The number is 5839161. My mother never ever speaks about that number and I never really noticed it until I was about four or five. Then one evening my mother was combing my hair and I kept watching the number going up and down, up and down. My eyes followed it all the time. So I asked her what it was but all she said was "Shush" or something. That night my dad came to tuck me in and I asked him. He said there are some things I shouldn't know about until I'm grown up. Irit— she's my older sister—has the room next to mine and so I sneaked in and asked her. She said that Germans—bad Germans—did it to our mother when she was a little girl in Poland. I didn't understand. I remember staying up thinking why should Germans want to draw 5839161 on my mother's arm. Then, one day, when my mother was combing my hair and I was watching the number going up and down, I began to cry and I couldn't stop crying. She held me tight, very tight, and she told me that one day, not now, she would explain what had happened to her when she was a little girl in Poland.

My parents still don't talk about it and I've stopped asking. One day we went from school with our teacher to Jerusalem to see Yad Vashem where they have that museum showing what the Nazis did to the Jews. That night I had nightmares. I just couldn't imagine my mother being treated like that, being made to do terrible things. I never said anything to her and I still try not to think about it much. I just don't know how to

33

think about it. But now that I'm older, I understand one thing. I understand why I never had any grandparents or uncles or aunts. They were all murdered by the Nazis. It's just us.

Israel's primordial monument to heroic tragedy rises out of the Judean desert in savage scenic isolation. It is called Masada, a precipice perched high above the Dead Sea. King Herod fashioned his famed winter palace out of its seemingly unscalable crags and, from its ramparts and balustrades, ancient Israel's fighters fought out their final hopeless battle against besieging Roman legions. For three years, between A.D. 70 and 73, nearly a thousand Jews held the Romans at bay until, debilitated and decimated, they chose mass suicide rather than surrender. Josephus, the historian of the day, records the Masada epic in hair-raising detail, projecting it as an apocalyptic

Within the ramparts of Masada deep in the Judean Desert: Israel's primordial monument to heroic tragedy.

convulsion of self-mutilation following the destruction of Jerusalem three years earlier when more than a million Jews had perished. Thus did the first holocaust unfold.

With the debacle of Masada the Roman stranglehold on the Jews tightened. One further spasm of valiant, violent, and initially successful revolt was throttled by a Roman assault so brutal as to devastate much of the land. With that, the almost two-thousand-year night of exile, of national eclipse, descended. In the family of nations "the Wandering Jew" became the stereotyped image. The dispersion spread and with it prejudice, poverty, persecution, and expulsion. At different times and in different places the sun of tolerance and opportunity shone, only to be darkened again by blind bigotry, pogrom, and banishment. This classic condition of Jewish homelessness and helplessness was destined, nineteen hundred years after Masada, to be repeated in the terrifying pit of the Nazi inferno. By the time those flames were extinguished, the ashes of six million Jews, a million and a half of them children, were left smoldering. Thus did the second holocaust unfold.

Both catastrophes, the ancient and the modern, have endowed the mount of Masada in the desert of Judea with profound meaning for Israel. It has become the symbol, noble and heroic, not of death, despair and defeat, but of defiant destiny. A contemporary oath declares: Masada shall not fall again. The words have acquired an almost psalmlike sanctity, a corollary to the biblical oath, "If I forget thee, O Jerusalem."

By tradition, recruits of Israel's armored corps climb the mount and, in solemn martial ceremony, swear allegiance to their colors affirming, "Masada shall not fall again." Youth-movement groups and school classes regularly make the steep serpentine ascent as a compulsory educational exercise in living history, an indoctrination in the Masada message that Israel's sovereignty shall never again be violated nor shall a genocide of Jews ever again occur.

So unambiguously does Israel see itself to be the progeny of the holocaust, the guarantor against its repetition, that the nation's Declaration of Independence of May 1948 states: "The catastrophe which recently befell the Jewish people—the massacre of millions of Jews in Europe—was another clear demonstration of the urgency of solving the problem of its homelessness by reestablishing in Eretz Israel the Jewish State which would open the gates of the Homeland wide to every Jew and confer upon the Jewish people the status of a fully privileged member of the community of nations."

(Overleaf) "Thus saith the Lord God unto these bones; behold, I will cause breath to enter into you, and Ye shall live"—Ezekiel 37.5.

On Mount Zion, Jerusalem, memorial plaques eulogize destroyed Jewish communities and a pillar of stone drips perpetual tears.

In the doctrine of Israel, the holocaust marked the watershed between past exilic persecution and future sovereign freedom.

Approximately one in five of Israel's population are holocaust survivors, hundreds of thousands are children of survivors, and many thousands live still with the light blue death-camp number tattooed on their arm. Given Israel's own history of struggle for survival, the memory—some would say the complex—of the holocaust is ever present near society's surface. Whenever outside threat has loomed, that memory has exposed itself like a raw nerve, the collective membrane twitching to the experience of Auschwitz.

Inscribed on the official state calendar is a Day of Kaddish, of recitation of the prayer for the dead, intoned by relatives in memory of their kin killed they know not when. There is another anniversary, observed nationwide, commemorating the mass extermination and the valor of the condemned. It is called Heroes and Martyrs Memorial Day, a whole twenty-four hours when all public entertainment shuts down, when flags are lowered to half-mast, and when sirens sound bringing traffic and people everywhere to a two-minute halt in silent homage to the six million dead. On that night and day, atop every public and government building, fiery red and yellow beacons shine, memorial candelabras illuminate the synagogues, and torches and pyres burn around each holocaust monument throughout the land.

On a hill overlooking Jerusalem stands Yad Vashem, which means simply the Monument. It is a vast complex of research centers and libraries documenting the name of every known victim, every community, every episode, every book, every piece of paper, indeed every recorded detail of the holocaust period. Here is located Israel's central museum of the carnage visually illustrating the phase by phase program of the liquidation of European Jewry. A Boulevard of Righteous Gentiles, lined with trees named in tribute to non-Jews who risked their lives to save Jews, leads to the cold stark concrete emptiness of the Memorial Tent where ashes from the crematoria are interred beneath giant flagstones inscribed with the names of the death camps, all illuminated by a single flame eternally burning. Year by year, on the eve of Heroes and Martyrs Memorial Day, as darkness descends, television and radio carry live the official ceremony of remembrance and dirge from the courtyard of Yad Vashem.

All countries have their day of memoriam for those who fell in battle. The State of Israel eulogizes a genocide.

It is perhaps because a catastrophe of such dimension has

Youngsters are brought up on the doctrine that the Jewish state is the historic answer to the holocaust.

39

never happened to a nation before that Israel's youngsters often find it hard to grasp. It is so mind-boggling that many simply are incapable of coming to grips with it, intellectually and emotionally. Born into the freedom of a Jewish state, they cannot know what Jewish homelessness was. Reared on the pride of Jewish self-defense, they cannot know what Jewish helplessness is. And having the means to defend their own flag they cannot know the feelings of a Jew without a flag. They can read, speculate, and wonder what the Jewish world was like before there was a Jewish state, but they can never know.

There was a time, in the early years of Israel's independence, when this blessed ignorance spawned questions that were outrageous. Not understanding, not knowing the facts, high on their own recently won independence against momentous odds, the youth were capable of the harshest judgments, pointing an accusing finger at the Jewish victims of Nazism for allowing themselves to drown in the bath of their own blood.

"I remember," recalls Jerusalem-born Techiya, herself now a mother of two, "what kind of questions we used to ask as teen-agers in the fifties when discussing the holocaust. We were arrogant. Don't forget, we were the first generation of the Jewish state and our own war of independence was still fresh in our minds. So the kind of classic question we asked was, How could they, the six million, have allowed themselves to be led like sheep to their own slaughter? Why didn't they fight back? We, too, were threatened in 1948, but we fought back. We were then only six hundred fifty thousand Jews surrounded by millions of Arabs. What did we have to defend ourselves—planes? tanks? artillery? The Arabs had whole armies and all we possessed were smuggled rifles and mortars with a few home-made cannons. But we stood up and we fought. We bled but we won. Why didn't they fight back? That was the big question we sabras asked in those days and I don't recall anybody giving us a really satisfactory answer until Adolf Eichmann came along."

On May 25, 1960, David Ben-Gurion, the then prime minister of Israel, mounted the rostrum of the Knesset to deliver an announcement. Adolf Eichmann, a leading planner and implementor of the Nazi holocaust of the Jews, had been tracked down in Argentina and abducted by Israeli agents to the Jewish state to be tried before a Jerusalem court. The news left Israel spellbound. Most significant was the explanation Ben-Gurion gave as to why he had ordered Eichmann's capture even at the risk of the diplomatic rupture with the government of Argentina which followed. Two days after his sensa-

(*Opposite*) A child's portrait of the holocaust.

(*Overleaf*) Section of a sculpture at Yad Vashem, Jerusalem. It is perhaps because a catastrophe of such dimension has never happened to a nation before that Israel's youngsters often find it hard to grasp.

tional Knesset revelation, Ben-Gurion wrote the following in a letter to a colleague: "To me, the significance of Eichmann's capture and his trial in Israel are not the skill and enterprise of our security services—magnificent though they be—but the privilege which is theirs in enabling an Israeli court to unveil the complete story of the holocaust so that the youth of Israel will finally learn the true facts and remember them, our youngsters who grew up after the holocaust and who, to this day, have heard but a faint echo of that unprecedented historic atrocity."

Adolf Eichmann's eight-month trial in Jerusalem is registered as the most significant, serious, and comprehensive judicial inquiry into the facts of the holocaust ever to have been undertaken anywhere. Witness after witness—more than a hundred in all—mounted the stand to give testimony to the extermination, the Nazi racial ideology that defined Jews as subhuman, the cunning and trickery that left whole communities unsuspecting as they were led to the gas chambers, the escapes, the cultural life even under the shadow of death, the ghettoizations, the resistance, the uprisings in the death camps, the Jewish partisans in the forests, and above all, the life and death of millions of Jews on another planet called Nazi Europe, a place so remote from human experience, let alone civilization, that none but those there could ever possibly understand. Never was a court case in Israel so thoroughly covered by the media.

In a profound sense Adolf Eichmann's trial became—as Ben-Gurion knew it must—a dramatic and sobering educational experience for the country's youth, enlightening them with answers to questions which only such a systematic judicial process could provide. To this day the trial is remembered not only for the justice it meted out to Adolf Eichmann (found guilty, he was hanged, his body cremated, and the ashes strewn over the Mediterranean) but, no less, for the moral justice it rendered to the memory of the six million in the eyes of the post-holocaust generation. It was as if the Jewish state had shaken off enough of the trauma to enable itself to stare hard into the hell that was and examine it agonizingly and clinically for what it was—a manmade, premeditated, planned slaughter of a people, not a demonic cataclysm unleashed by Satans beyond the forces of nature.

From that day forth Israeli research into the holocaust period was given significant impetus. Educators experimented—not very successfully—with techniques to translate the historiography of the holocaust into a language understandable to sabras. The purpose was

(*Opposite*) Year by year Yad Vashem attracts ever larger numbers of youngsters who ask fewer critical questions but want to know more facts.

not only to induce a sense of identification and a knowledge of the facts but also, on a deeper level, to inculcate a feeling of responsibility as to the role of the Jewish state in the post-holocaust Jewish world.

One third of world Jewry perished between 1939 and 1945. The six million who were exterminated were the elite. It is estimated that eighty percent of Jewry's greatest teachers, writers, scholars, spiritual leaders, and artists died in the gas chambers. The centers of learning which the Nazis destroyed in Europe had, for centuries, served as the Harvards and Princetons of the Jewish people, the cultural, religious core of Jewish life everywhere. The rise of Israel out of the ashes of the holocaust invested the Jewish state with the responsibility of keeping the Jewish people alive on the stage of history. This was the single consolation. Israel alone was the guarantor that the Jewish body would cease to be bled and the Jewish spirit would cease to be sapped away into the oblivion of assimilation. Israel defined its own destiny as the carrier, physical and cultural, of the Jewish heritage. Were the Jewish state to go, the Jewish people would die.

This being the stated creed, it is amazing how difficult it has been for Israel's educational system to digest the study of the holocaust. Countless seminars over many years failed to come up with a credible formula. Until well into the 1960s the history of the holocaust was treated in the high schools as one chapter of the regular Jewish history course, meaning that many a high school student graduated without having managed to cover all the material as far as 1939. An educational reform was introduced and the holocaust was recognized as an elective matriculation project. But again relatively few pupils chose the option since too few had the time to cover the study in depth. For the most part, it was squeezed into the classroom one week a year, the spring week between Heroes and Martyrs Memorial Day and Independence Day. Apart from that and some lessons on literature, the study was virtually ignored.

In a country where the holocaust has been so manifestly institutionalized, where so many of its citizens are holocaust survivors, and which so dramatically links itself to the holocaust experience, this gap in formal education has been outrageous. It was not until 1979 that the Ministry of Education issued a publication, *Innovations in the Educational System for the School Year 1979–1980,* and wrote: "In the 1979–1980 school year the Ministry of Education will implement its decision to teach the holocaust as a compulsory subject in all high schools. This decision was taken after consultations with officials of

Yad Vashem, researchers, and public representatives. The decision to introduce the study of the holocaust as a compulsory subject was adopted after it became clear that under the existing high school curricula a student can complete all his grades without sufficient knowledge (and often with no knowledge at all) of the holocaust period."

Yael, a petite, dark-haired, brown-eyed twelfth-grade student in a high school for girls in Jerusalem, pondered why it took more than thirty years to get such a curriculum moving: "I honestly think it's taken this long for the country to distance itself enough to see it all in perspective. It is, after all, a highly charged subject. From all that I've learned, the Eichmann trial was a kind of turning point but it's taken another twenty years to bring the subject down from the level of academic research into the high school. Our school was one of the first in which the new program was tried out."

And what of its effectiveness?

"It's mind-blowing. We were taught the facts as they were without embellishment and after every lesson we walked away with the question, how would we have reacted? What would we have done in the Lodz ghetto and the Warsaw ghetto? What would we have thought about at night in Treblinka and Auschwitz? We had no answers. There are none. There is just no way of understanding how anyone survived. Those who did must have been superhuman. We learned about daily life under the Nazis—what people wore in the ghettos and concentration camps, what they wrote, what work children were forced to do, what they ate, what kind of cultural life was possible, things like that. The people became alive as real people before they died and before we kind of died with them. We also looked at the holocaust in its political context, in the context of the war as a whole. The most horrible realization of all, as far as I'm concerned, is that the Allies knew, the British and the Americans knew it was all happening yet they did nothing to stop the slaughter. That I cannot forgive. I blame the world as much as I blame the Nazis for the murder of the six million Jews."

And what are Yael's conclusions?

"Israel is the only hope, the only guarantee that it won't happen again. We won't let it. This is what I feel. That, and the responsibility to remember. We must always remember actively, consciously, so that the next generations of Israelis will know. We must pass it on. I don't want my own grandchildren to look upon the holocaust as I look upon the Inquisition of the Jews in Spain in 1492, as something remote and abstract."

And what of Germany today?

"Actually, I would like to visit Germany, I would like to see the people who did that to our people. This might sound silly but I would like to see them and I would want them to see me—me, alive, a kid from the Jewish state. It would, I think, give me a kind of satisfactory revenge."

Yael's words reflect the resolve of the educational authorities to finally come to grips, inside the classroom, with what has proven to be the most difficult of subjects, and to teach it not just as history but as heritage. Jews lived in Europe for one thousand years. The forebears of hundreds of thousands of Israeli youngsters stem from cities, towns, and villages—now empty of Jews—through which the holocaust rolled. They have to know. However, what of that other sector of Israeli-born youth—the majority—whose roots are not European (Ashkenazic) but Middle Eastern and North African (Sephardic)? They, too, are a part of the collective Israeli heritage and they, too, must know. Yet rendering the holocaust comprehensible to them is even more difficult, for their history within the Moslem world was so different from that of European Jewry in the Christian world. With all the checkered episodes of inequality and pogrom which Sephardic Jews suffered there is no Sephardic recollection of holocaust. Moreover, the difficulty of teaching the story of the European catastrophe to these youngsters has always been compounded by their own perceptions of Ashkenazic ethnocentricity and the self-image it has engendered.

Idit, a dark, delicate-looking beauty, completed her high-schooling with exceptional grades as a flautist at the Jerusalem Academy of Music. This is how she reflects upon the problem:

"I must have been nine or ten years old, in the fourth or fifth grade, when our teachers first spoke to us about the holocaust. I didn't understand a thing. Every now and again, during the course of the years, we had a further lesson or two but they hardly captured our imagination. When you are that young, there are any number of lessons one has to sit through under duress and I suspect that for most of us the holocaust was one of them. It was so remote, so unreal, just another tragic chapter in history, and I never even really understood what century it happened in. Only much later did I begin to conceive the absolute horror of the holocaust, and so absolute is it that even now I don't pretend to understand. It's simply beyond human comprehension. Never at any time in school was the subject presented to us in a systematic, structured fashion in depth, within a context of time and space we could grasp. It was always treated in a kind of limbo, as if in a vacuum, resurrected every now and again when the memorial anniversary came around. This was compounded by a teacher who was himself the son of a survivor so that his presentations were emotional, without interpretation. What made the experience even more grotesque was the fact that, for me, Europe was another world, foreign and strange. My family's roots are in Iraq and I resented the fact that it was always European Jewry we were learning about, hardly ever Middle Eastern Jewry. I knew that so much of Jewish scholarship, philosophy, and culture derived from the ancient communities of North Africa and the Middle East but apart from some medieval poetry this hardly figured in our lessons. To me it was almost like discrimination. It was enough to give one an inferiority complex. Kids of Ashkenazic origin seemed to have a much sharper sense of self-identity than we youngsters of Sephardic origin and it created a gap between us. Which is another reason, an important reason, why I found it so hard to identify with the holocaust of the European Jews. Today it's different, but those were my feelings only a few years ago and I blame the school. As one gets older, one cannot live in Israel without absorbing a sensitivity toward the holocaust. So many went through it and so much has happened here with regard to our own security problems to influence the thinking and the behavior of people. The point is that I believe we youngsters of Sephardic origin would have a much readier ear to learn about the holocaust in school were it presented in a context that did not somehow diminish our own pride in our own origins as Sephardic Jews."

Speaking to children whose parents actually experienced the holocaust one senses involuntary suppression. Invariably, the parents themselves were but youngsters when the horror rolled over them and many a survivor does not volunteer all that much to the children. It would also appear that numerous youngsters prefer not to personalize their parents' past. No young person can be expected to handle with equanimity the imagery of one's mother or father reduced to an animallike existence in a camp of death. Parent-child relationships in such families have their hidden moods, precious passions, and unique bonds of protection, possessiveness, responsibility, and love.

Ilan, a lanky, curly-headed sixteen-year old from the southern port town of Eilat, whose father is an Auschwitz survivor, tells it thus: "At home nobody wants to speak about the holocaust. I've grown up with an awareness, of course, but with no real knowledge. The first time I ever felt anything was last year. It was a strange experience. It was the morning of Heroes and Martyrs Memorial Day and I was on my way to school. The siren sounded. Everything stopped, cars, and people, everything. Men and women stood in the street in silence and I honestly felt embarrassed. I tried to feel something but nothing came. Except for the wailing noise of the siren there was a deadly hush and the only thing that came into my mind was next week's exam. I remember whispering to myself words like 'Auschwitz,' 'gas chambers,' 'six million,' but they were just empty phrases. Then, across the street, my eye caught an old man—he looked like a Russian immigrant—leaning against a wall. He wore a battered brown hat, baggy trousers, and his shirt was gray. In his hand he clutched a string shopping bag containing a loaf of bread. He just stood there, looking straight ahead, expressionless. Suddenly, I felt it—the holocaust. That man to me was the picture of the whole thing. I just knew he was mourning his own dead, his own suffering. For the first time in my life I felt something; I had the strange sensation that I had rid myself of some inexplicable guilt complex. I could finally associate the holocaust to my own father even if I couldn't talk to him about it."

Seventeen-year-old Davina, who lives in Herzliya, a resort town north of Tel Aviv, reflects on her relationship with her parents, both of whom went through the camps. Haltingly and thoughtfully she says: "My father has one older brother in America—my uncle Shimon—but my mother lost everybody. They met in Israel after the war. My father entered the country legally during the time of the

The last march to the crematoria: The children learn that among the millions who perished were the cultural elite of their people.

War sculpture by Tamarkin. Nothing has galvanized this nation more than the folk-feeling that in defending the country its people were protecting their children from yet another holocaust.

British rule, but my mother was on the *Exodus,* that refugee ship that tried to run the British blockade but was caught and sent back to Germany. After the State was declared in 1948, she returned and joined the same kibbutz youth group as my father. That's how they met and married. As long as I can remember, I have grown up with the feeling that things in our house are different. Neither of my parents has ever spoken much about what they went through. Me and my older brother and sister, Misha and Avital, sometimes speak about what it must have been like, but we don't really know. I honestly can't think of my parents in terms of the crematoria. I sometimes look at my mother and wonder, Did they beat her, did they make her do terrible things? She never has told us and I'll never ask. And I look at my father and think about those pictures of boys sorting the clothes of the dead. Was he one of those boys? I don't know; I don't want to know. It was as if both my parents had slammed a door on a past too terrible to talk about. Once, on the beach, a group of young German tourists pitched their sun tent close to ours. My father said, 'Let's move,' and without a word my mother got up and began collecting the things. I said, 'Why? Can't you stand even seeing them?' And my mother said, 'Let's move.' But I wanted an answer. I wanted to understand what they felt. So I said, 'Those people were too young to have been involved—they weren't born when the war was on.' 'I know,' replied my father. 'You're right. But let's move just the same.' He spoke with such finality that there was nothing I could say. Their own youth is all sealed and beyond reach. They will never allow any of us to enter that door, never."

Occasionally something explodes in Israel that jerks the senses into memory, an incident that is so nakedly reminiscent of heinous scenes of the past as to awaken the sleeping fears even of the youth. Such has been the case when PLO terrorists—significantly branded by official spokesmen as the "SS Arabs"—have seized schoolchildren as hostages, or babies in a nursery, surrounding their cribs with explosives. In the minds of many, such atrocity compels association with another time and place when Jewish babies were smashed to death. Whenever a terrorist action has chosen children for hostage, the nation has tensed in anticipation for what everybody knows must happen: rescue. This, above all, was the imperative that led to Entebbe.

In 1976 an Air France jet en route from Tel Aviv to Paris was hijacked by Arab terrorists under the command of a German sympathizer. The aircraft was forced to land at Entebbe, Uganda, ruled then by Idi Amin. What sent the coldest shiver down the Israeli spine was the news that the German commander had released all non-Jews and had kept the Jews, children included, as hostages. In the eyes of the Jewish state that "selection" was Auschwitz all over again. Jews were being selected for killing only because they were Jews. The Israeli government ordered the army to prepare for and launch a rescue mission that was to lift across a continent a large commando force in the dead of night and, by stealth and subterfuge, occupy the Entebbe airfield and bring the hostages home. To the youth of Israel, it was the ultimate answer to the helplessness that made the holocaust. It was as if this people were subjecting every tissue and sinew in its body to a test almost beyond reason to prove to themselves and to the world that had there been a Jewish state in 1939, six million could never have been exterminated. In the words of one of the rescued hostages: "I didn't know how and I didn't know when but as God is my witness I knew, I just knew, that our army would come and save us. It had to. No matter the odds and whatever the cost, the Israeli forces had to get us out. If Israel ever had meaning and a purpose after the holocaust, it was proven at Entebbe."

Natan, a fifteen-year-old boy from Beersheba, put it in verse this way:

> I wonder if in days gone by,
> Six million Jews would have had to die.
> Had Israel existed, so Entebbe proves,
> Our army would have saved our Jews.

This sentiment seems to say it all. It illustrates the perspective in which young Israelis instinctively perceive the holocaust in the context of their own experience. In the words of Yael, whose school helped pioneer the program of holocaust studies: "This is what we concluded was the most important thing of all—perspective. Through our studies we understood that it is wrong, in a Jewish sense, to make the holocaust the central experience of modern Jewish history. It is not. It must be seen in the perspective of all our history. Now that the country is old enough to look at it with some dispassion, we must stop sentimentalizing it. That makes it vulgar. Remember and mourn, yes. Hitler killed more than all the other anti-Semites of the past only because he had the scientific means to do so. But the attempt to destroy our people is not new. From Pharaoh on down this is a recurrent theme of our history. This is the perspective. Because of it, Israel's obsession with its security makes moral sense. That's what the holocaust means to me."

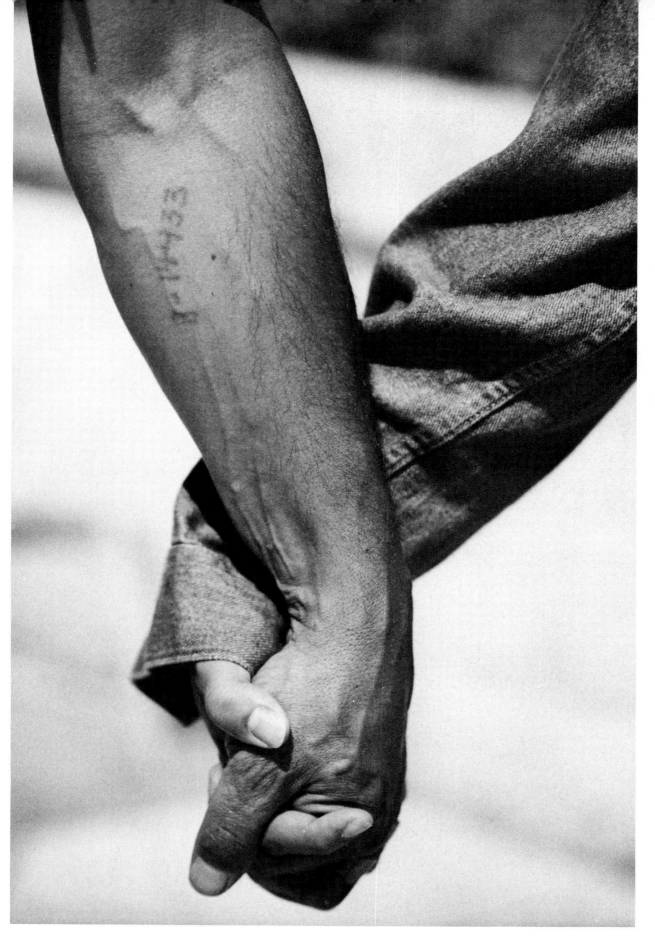

III

The Cactus Kids

Ezer, Aged Seventeen, Ahuza, Haifa

When it comes to pronouncing big words, people my age don't like it; we get embarrassed. I mean words like patriotism and national duty and service to the country—it's not our style. We don't put our feelings on public display and we're not given to parading our emotions in front of others. The high-sounding ideological Zionist slogans just bore us. Either you live it or you don't. If you're born here and have had any semblance of a decent education, then you do what you have to do. You do it with conviction, without fuss. Old-timers are forever telling us how great they were when they were our age and visitors from abroad are forever preaching about how important Israel is for the survival of the Jewish people. Fine. If it's that important, why don't they come here? This country wasn't built on speeches. That's putting it bluntly but this is how most kids my age feel. People sometimes say that we're too outspoken, too noisy, a pretty rude lot in fact. I don't think we are. We do have this habit of saying what we think. But what's wrong with that? At least it's honest. I guess it has something to do with our upbringing. I also suspect it has something to do with the life here; by the time we're eighteen, we're expected to carry a hell of a lot on our shoulders. We don't have the time to laze around or go in for all that guru stuff like young people in America. I sometimes wish we did. But I wouldn't want to change things. They say it's good for youth to have to face challenges. If so, we suffer no shortage of them here. They're real. Don't think we're practicing idealists, or some-

thing like that. We're not. It's just that this little country is all we have, and to be born here—well, it's kind of a responsibility to be a sabra.

Nobody remembers who concocted the nickname but it has stuck: To be born and bred in Israel is to be labeled sabra. It means cactus, that wild, prickly, sunbaked, tough plant which flourishes in the arid earth and produces a fruit deliciously soft and sweet.

This is how the early pioneers idealistically imagined the future generations of Israeli youth: free and strong and proud, tough on the outside, sensitive within, bronzed by the sun of nascent Israel and unscarred by the aberrations of the twentieth-century exile. To be a sabra, they rhapsodized, was to be the new Jew, liberated, born out of the earth where Jewish history began. The title hinted at resilience and fortitude: pioneer against desert, few against many, vision against reality, David against Goliath.

Who were those pioneers, the founding fathers of modern Israel? They were turn-of-the-century idealists, the sons and daughters of the ugly cramped Jewish ghettos and of the impoverished shtetls,

Youth movements have a long tradition nurtured by the pioneer mystique.

A kindergarten class. Education is the largest item of the national budget, next to defense.

the shanty hamlets of eastern Europe where generations of anti-Semitism had pogrommed the Jewish body but could not bleed the Jewish soul. They were the children of "Fiddler on the Roof" communities, nurtured on Talmudic dialectic and on Hassidic messianic visions which, when catalyzed by the secular nationalistic fervors of the day, triggered a revolution called Zionism. They, a few hundred followed later by a few thousand, turned their backs on the swift-flowing migrant waves that cascaded across the Atlantic from the old Diaspora to the new and, instead, obstinately channeled their own rivulet back toward ancient Zion. Such were the early pioneers. They were going home to rebuild a New Jerusalem, reclaim the national birthright, renounce the exile, revive the Hebrew language, and restore the Land of Israel to its scattered children. These were the themes of the poems and songs they composed, the ideology of their speeches, the subjects of their literature and deeds.

"Revolutionaries, that's what we were, revolutionaries," declares Matti, one of the last of the old-timers who set out on foot from a Ukrainian Jewish hamlet in 1912 en route for the Promised Land. Matti doesn't trust his legs anymore and arthritis has locked his old leathery hands. But his white hair is still bountiful and his eyes are dashingly blue, and when he reminisces, he tends to bark with bari-

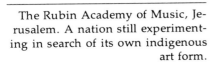

The Rubin Academy of Music, Jerusalem. A nation still experimenting in search of its own indigenous art form.

tone authority. His home is a single room overlooking Rothschild Boulevard in the Tel Aviv hostelry reserved for founder senior citizens. "Look at it," he snarls, pointing from his rocking chair strategically placed on the balcony facing the traffic-jammed tree-lined street below. "Look what's become of Tel Aviv. I remember it when it was a few streets, a dusty shack of a town hall and over there, where that skyscraper is, there were tents and huts. Those were the sandy outskirts. Now it's all inner city: no camels, no mules, no carriages, just cars and buses and taxis. I once had a journalist come to see me from somewhere and he said to me the old days here must have been something like those of the American frontier pioneers. Poppycock, I said. Those Americans who went west had no ideology. They were individualists, tough ones and rugged, on the march for whatever pastures they could find. Not us. We were revolutionaries. We came out here to make a revolution together. Our relatives left the shtetls and ghettos of Poland and Russia and went to America. Not us. We weren't looking for bread. We were going home. We had ideology, beliefs, that's what we had. No more Diaspora for us, we said. We were going to change ourselves, make ourselves into farmers and build a whole new decent society out of nothing. We were going to take Hebrew out of the prayer book and bring it back to life. We were going to build our own army and have our own flag after two thousand years. That, my friend, is a revolution! My God, how

63

we dreamed, how we sweated, how we sang and danced. We had come back home to Eretz Israel and we never stopped singing how beautiful we were going to make it."

For Matti and his generation, those who began draining the marshlands, reclaiming the desert, and creating unique patterns of rural living like the kibbutz and the moshav, the future was a beckoning horizon of messianic promise toward which they labored with fierce self-sacrifice. They fueled their souls with the ideological ardor of national revival. Their passion for the dogma of their envisioned utopia produced inner debate of tumultuous exuberance.

Prominent in that debate was the new generation. The founding fathers and mothers were going to breed wondrous offspring who would inherit the utopia. Out of the rock, sand, and soil of Zion would spring the sabra. He would be different. He would turn inside out and upside down the ghetto-shtetl stereotype into which centuries of persecution had molded the Jew. The sabra would tear to pieces the anti-Semite's portrait of the groveling, money-grubbing, cunning Shylock wandering the ghetto alleyways with his mean trade and craft. No longer would the Jews be wandering; they would be planting. No longer would they be fleeing; they would be defending. No longer would they be pale, frail, and frightened but erect, muscular, and fighting. Every trait, every custom, every characteristic that ghetto life had branded onto the flesh of the ghetto child was to be exorcised and washed clean by the sun, soil, and toil of the new Israel in which the sabra would germinate. This was the dream and they

Tel Aviv news vendor earning pocket money before going to school.

Sitting on the fence at the weekend football match. For most modern-day youth the revolution is over.

deliberated long, hard, and loudly on the kind of schools they would build, the type of teacher they would muster, and the techniques they would employ to impart to their children an inheritance of patriotism and service, physical labor and enterprise, independence of spirit and freedom of soul. Oh, how they toiled and sacrificed to build the new Zion out of its desolation, raped and ravished by the erosion of time; how certain they were that out of this reborn Zion would come forth the new Jew, the new identity, the sabra.

Seventy years later the original prototype still lingers on in the national mystique though weathered, faded, and mellowed by the passage of time. The fire of the romantic idealism has spent itself, for much of the ideal has been achieved. The pioneer passion has abated, for much of the pioneer toil has been done. The rural egalitarian ideology has lost its aggressive thrust, for most of the population is now urbanized. Finally, the sabra prototype has lost much of its novelty, for it is fashioned now by a consumer competitive society which seeks whatever good things affluence may offer. What is left is a potent nostalgia leavened by an abiding patriotism and spiced by a goodly portion of sabra "chutzpa."

By any measure, Israel's mainstream native-born adolescents remain rather cactuslike: earthy, tough, exuberant, brusque, cliquish, very short on manners, and prone to a sentimentality which they try hard to mask. They carry with them from the past a vernacular that is atrociously stark and inordinately unemotional. Since Hebrew enshrines too few seedy words, they are compelled to resort to Arabic for coarse language. Though they are Mediterranean, their behavior is dispassionate and even their love vocabulary is notoriously unimaginative. To resort to emotional superlatives is to be soft, and that is the last thing the sabra wants to appear.

Israel was and remains an intensely youth-oriented society. Its youngsters grow up under an adult-focused microscope that magnifies every detail that does not fit society's image of itself. It was never different. It was not long before the founder pioneers began to find fault with their own first sabra generation for not measuring up to their superlative parental image. Israel's pilgrim fathers were an elite, after all. They were self-selected, having voluntarily transplanted body and soul to a barren, inhospitable geography, there to mix sweat with soil and deliberately change, through social and national resurrection, the course of Jewish history from dependence to independence. As for their children, they had no particular penchant for revolutionary passion. They were what their seniors had made them. They were not select. They were not driven. Their origins were not in the asphyxiating, complex-ridden atmosphere of the ghetto and shtetl but in the open hills and dales of Galilee and Judea. They were not persecuted tailors and Talmudists who had chosen to embrace manual labor as an ideology, as a source of spiritual elation worthy of song and dance. They were sabras. For them the backbreaking agricultural work of those early days was part of the scheme of things, often more of a drudgery than an idealistic self-liberation. And so the elders would bemoan the "ideological emptiness" of their growing youth, even as they basked in their bronzed virgin-peasant, gentile-looking muscular physiques. They were, indeed, a new breed of Jews.

What time was to prove, what it has always proved, is not that the youth were worse than their elders: they were different. In the extraordinary circumstances of contemporary Israel, the test of time has always had a measure—the struggle for national survival. For generation after generation this, above all, is what has spanned the gap between generations.

Founders and sons clasped hands as the battle for self-determination and independence escalated. The assignment of the young, even teen-agers, was to volunteer for the crack underground defense units, to spearhead the watchtower and stockade frontier settlements,

(*Preceding pages*) To the pioneers the sabra was to be the New Jew, born out of the scenery of the ancient homeland.

to serve as the blockade runners, and ultimately, to become the young officers of the War of Independence, 1948. This was the sabra generation of Yitzhak Rabin, Moshe Dayan, Yigael Yadin, Yigael Allon, Ezer Weizman, Ariel Sharon. Thousands of their comrades fell in the struggle. A poet of the day was to describe them as "the silver platter" on which the Jewish state was presented to the Jewish people. To these youngsters Israel owed its birth. It was a youth that acquitted itself astonishingly.

Then came the next generation, the post-Independence youth, those who grew up in the 1950s and 1960s. They lived in the shadow of the legends of both the founders and the sons. It was as if they had been born two days after the tempestuous, lofty, intellectual revolution of their grandparents and a day after their parents had fought and won the battle of independence. They were the generation of the new state and they faced something of a dilemma. The success of

their elders had turned most of the dream into a daily reality. What was there left to do? Where before there had been a grand cause embracing a whole community of volunteers, now there was officialdom. Everything became institutionalized, organized, and directed from above by a bureaucracy governed not by vision but by laws, not by idealism but by reality. These sabras were now enjoined to conform to the mechanisms of continuity as prescribed by, and embodied in, the institutions of statehood. The revolution was over.

Not that the national tasks were done, they were just beginning. But it was not what it used to be. The drama, the challenge wasn't the same. To this generation, the word *Zionism* lost its rhetorical punch. Ben-Gurion, one of the revolutionary pioneers and then the prime minister, was furious. The Negev was still a desert, he thundered, the Galil was still empty. Go out and build the waste places, he challenged. He even set a personal example by establishing

Childhood in Israel is what healthy childhood anywhere should mean: play and school and chores and make-believe and mischief and as jolly a time as can be had.

The older they become, the more they talk about what they are going to do in the army.

his home in a fledgling Negev kibbutz. But few listened and even fewer followed. In anger he hurled at them what was possibly the worst insult he could command: "Careerists!" That word, in the pre-State days, meant selfish pursuit of personal ambition rather than voluntary subordination to the priorities of the community. It was the ultimate calumny. Yizhar, a prominent writer, labeled this post-Independence youth the "espresso generation"—quick, bitter, cheap. In a learned paper a psychologist suggested that "our children are ashamed to be ashamed, are afraid to be afraid. They are afraid to love, are afraid to give of themselves. I am not sure whether it is a deficiency in emotion or being afraid of feeling." The sabras were in the dock and they were found grossly wanting.

The chorus of criticism ended abruptly in the summer of 1967. A test of time had come. Those who were the children of the fifties and the teen-agers of the sixties—"the espresso generation"—were now the fighters of the Six Day War. Parents stood anxious and amazed, moved and humbled at the spectacle of their sabra soldier sons flinging themselves into the battle in a desperate bid to rescue Israel from yet another threat of destruction. Their war of '67 was more, far more, than a baptism of fire. For those who had grown up

in the new state and who had taken its existence for granted, the war was a terrifying shock treatment driving home the realization that for survival's sake nothing in Israel dare be taken for granted. They mourned their dead and nursed their wounds, coming home from battle with no sense of victory, only salvation. They showed that they hated war with a passion; they showed that they would defend their land with a passion. In a volume called *The Seventh Day*, they recorded their individual and collective thoughts in writing, a rare testimony to their humanity, beliefs, self-questioning, resources, and

"Our youngsters don't have all that many years to be young."

Jewish heritage. Never before had this generation so articulated its soul. The nation had grossly misjudged them. Now it was indebted, relieved, thankful, proud. In the words of the influential kibbutz journal, *Shdemot:* "It seemed that the harmony between the parents and the children had been restored. Continuity between the generations was reestablished, expressed in courage and sacrifice. Once again there was a link between the grandparents—the builders of the country, the parents—the liberators of the country, and the sons—the saviors of the country, the heroes of the Six Day War."

Sabras are not quite
the breed the pioneers
envisioned, although a good
many of them come fairly
close to the image.

Six years later it happened again—the surprise attack on Yom Kippur. That war proved to be the most grueling test of them all, engulfing the sabras who had been the school kids of the sixties and early seventies. They held back the onslaught and bought critical time for the experienced civilian reserve to mobilize and turn what looked like disaster into victory. It was their turn to defend and they did, ferociously.

And so to the youngsters of today. Soon they will graduate from school and be called upon to mount the watch. How do they feel? What do they say?

"We don't talk about our feelings much but there isn't one among us who doesn't talk about what we want to do in the army." The voice belongs to Danny, turned seventeen and approaching his last high school year. A studious, soft-spoken lad, he sits with some friends on the steps of the Boy Scout clubhouse in the Valley of the Cross, Jerusalem. "We sabras can't be like American or English kids when we know that next year we're going into the army. Our prayer is we won't have to fight. I'm no hero—who is? But I know, most of us know, that when it comes to it we'll volunteer for a crack unit because that's the right thing to do. None of us likes to preach patriotism; we just know what we're supposed to do. It's not easy. It's not easy when we are supposed to be manly before we are men and be unafraid when there's something to fear. For most of us, I think, going into the army is not to win wars but to prevent them. Egypt made peace with us because Sadat knew he couldn't beat us. That's what the army's for and that's the only way the others are going to make peace if at all. I know that some people here think that we sabras are beginning to get soft. Maybe we are. God help the country if it's true."

Since the days of Socrates, youth has been preached to and reproached for failing to be what an older generation has decided they should become. In Israel, the charge once was that the youngsters had no ideology, then that they had no idealism, that they didn't have enough patriotism, and now some contend they are overly materialistic, are getting soft.

Tehilla is quick to challenge the thought. Tehilla is fair-haired, blue-eyed, and cast in the sleek sabra mold so cherished by Israel's matriarchs. "Look," she says, "look around you. This country can't live forever like a kibbutz. We're a modern industrial state and our grandfathers' ideals just don't apply. They had their dreams; we have ours. They had to do everything themselves. We have a government, a Knesset, an establishment. Sure, when we go off to enjoy the good things in life some leaders and politicians raise their hands in horror and moan about the lack of pioneering values. I think that's funny. Where else in the world do you find ninety percent of the kids going into the army for three years and more without making a fuss about it? We take it for granted. We don't like it, but it's part of growing up in this country and we know why we have to do it. That's the important thing—we still know why."

"Getting soft?" says Haim heatedly. "Who the hell can get soft in this country the way things are?" Haim is a chubby chap with an Afro and a rather loud voice. "I think that the rest of the world is making us into better Jews, better patriots, if that's the right word. Whenever I hear the United Nations say that Zionism is racism, or that we have to give up Jerusalem, I become a more convinced Israeli. Every week somebody else condemns us for something. For what? For existing, that's for what—for living, for being a Jewish state. The world could do without us. Sure there are differences of opinion among us—about the Arabs, and security and the borders and the

Look into the eyes of many a child and you see the reflection of a nation that is normal enough but somehow different.

settlements. This is only natural. We're a democracy. But I sometimes think that whatever we do, whatever concessions we'd make, it wouldn't make a damned difference. We'd still be condemned for something or other. That gets me mad. You don't have to be an old pioneer to want to defend this country. All you have to do is feel Jewish. If that means getting soft, then I'm soft."

Whatever legitimacy there might be to Haim's outrage—and there are teachers who say they do detect echoes of this sentiment in their classrooms—it is a fact that Israeli parents have become more ambitious for their children in the industrialized consumer society Israel has become. Material expectations are higher and so is the compulsion for higher education. Consequently, compared to previous generations, the youth are probably more indulged in the middle-class progression toward the good things of life. Moreover, the closer the youngsters approach the age of the draft, the more indulgent parents become.

A professional opinion on today's sabra is offered by Sima, a Tel Aviv secondary school teacher whose thoughts have the authority of more than twenty years' experience. "Remember," she says, "our youngsters don't have all those many years to be young. What psychologists sometimes call the 'adolescence moratorium' hardly exists

It is only in the later teens that the boys and girls pair off.

in Israel. There just isn't the time. Once a youngster reaches high school age there is no way he can indulge in building castles in the air. The army period is just around the corner. Very few talk about what they want to be as adults, or what they want to study in university. All of them talk about what they want to be in the army. This is their overriding concern, not career, not ambition, not study. They just don't have a time to dream. The only thing they can see ahead of them is the military service. To them it's not a problem; they see it as a natural duty. So among themselves they talk about it in typical sabra fashion by scoffing at their own patriotism or laughing at their own fears or joking about who has a better survival chance, the pilot or the parachutist. I sometimes think they are saying to each other we must be ready to die at eighteen and begin living again at twenty-one. 'Self-eulogy' is what they call it. They are good at telling sick

jokes against themselves: 'See you on the memorial tablet,' that kind of thing. Oh yes, they feel strongly about many things and they communicate their sentiments in their own way. Given the Israeli reality, sabras don't make good flower children or hippies. Considering the pressures around them and what's expected of them I think our sabras are amazingly adjusted and well-equipped to cope. All in all, they're a happy, independent lot. Teaching them can be hard at times but it's never boring."

Cactus kids like to live up to their image. They take pride in thinking themselves casual and cool. It's part of their education. From a relatively early age they, girls and boys, learn to rough it. All schools and youth organizations take them on hikes along mountain tracks and desert trails that must be exhausting for all but the toughest. Parents are invariably glad to see them go and even gladder to

Sabra pastimes: The youth have their own chess league; cubecatching is the Israeli equivalent of jacks; and basketball is a national sport.

see them back safe; the return home from these excursions—some of which can last for days, the kids sleeping in the open air—is frequently the cause for palpable relief. It is not unexceptional for the radio to announce that a certain named group is stuck out in the wilds somewhere and will not be back at the appointed hour. "So parents, not to worry." For the tired, dusty kids these outings are enjoyable stamina and confidence builders which, over the years, instill a knowledge and a love of the country and the countryside.

Sabras habitually like doing things together in groups, as though driven by some herd instinct. They usually prefer their own company, pursuing their recreation collectively. It is only in the later teens that they may, perhaps, unabashedly pair off. To openly display romance beforehand is "schmaltzy."

Sabra dress is simple always. Boys are never seen in a jacket and tie or girls adorned with anything more than a touch of makeup, if that. There is a kind of code about this, born out of the climate and the pioneer folklore. For reasons never explained the summer shorts fashion which once every self-respecting teen-age sabra paraded in the forties and fifties has vanished. In dress, sabras have become cosmopolitan: Jeans and T-shirts are now the norm.

Hair can be of every shape and length, though the general style is moderate. Perhaps this has something to do with the impending army haircut. Most girls seem to strive for the silky, long shoulder-

Sabras are big "noshers."

length-plus variety. To fathers, at least, daughters appear to invest an enormous amount of brushing time merely to keep the mane straight.

Tastes in music range anywhere from American jazz to Israeli pop to the lilting notes of native folk compositions. Symphony goers will find a remarkably large number of youngsters sprinkled about concert halls. Sabra adolescents are not great disco addicts and folk dancing is still a popular pastime for many.

Israelis work a six-day week, leaving the Sabbath as the only day for recreation—to watch a game, lounge on the beach, or play in the park.

As for sports, soccer and basketball are sacrosanct.

Sabras are big "noshers." Most of them seem to be eating something most of the time. Friday eve and Sabbath are regular bonanzas dedicated to the mass public consumption of *garinim*—roasted sunflower seeds that are systematically and nonchalantly cracked between the teeth, the spent gray shells spat forth for others to sweep up. Every stadium is carpeted with them at the close of the weekend match.

Weekdays, the kiosks and other "nosh" emporiums are open to all and downtown is busy with street snacks. Menus are munificent. The rage used to be *felafel*, that spicy, oriental delicacy of fried ground chick-pea balls, topped with salad and packaged in an envelope of *pitta*, Arab bread. Today, with the further blossoming of the sabra street-snack culture, the variety includes corn-on-the-cob, pizza, kosher Wimpys, quickie steaks, and even kosher Kentucky Fried Chicken. One enterprising Tel Aviv purveyor, expert in the sabra "nosh" palate, has been inspired by the name McDonald's to open a McDavid's. Also doing rather well are British fish-and-chips.

Sabras don't seem to seek their kicks in drugs. Some do, of course, but their problem has never spread to become a national epidemic. The complaint of Western youth about the curse of "dehumanizing technology" threatening to bulldoze personalities away that impels so many to pack up and leave in search of purpose—little of this has ever invaded the sabra soul. Evidently, the overwhelming majority finds no compelling need to experiment and escape. Escaping from anything in Israel is not easy. The country is too small. One cannot disappear into hills or vanish into concrete urban labyrinths or hide away in far-off retreats to get lost in esoteric subcultures. Anonymity is a terribly difficult thing to come by in Israel. Not only is there no place; there is virtually no time. For just at that age when frustration might storm tranquillity, precisely then does the *bagrut* loom, the all-important university-entrance exam. Even if one drops out of that, there is the army ahead. Only three years later (two for most girls) can one think of beginning studies or a career, by which time marriage becomes a consideration. Israelis do tend to marry young and establish their families early. It is no wonder, therefore, that Israeli universities never experienced the kind of excessive student convulsions that rocked the campuses of America and Western Europe. They remain relatively quiescent places dedicated to the single proposition of finishing studies as quickly as possible. Then, at last, the average sabra can get on with the actual job of normal living.

(Opposite) The cactus—wild, prickly, sunbaked, tough, with a deliciously soft inner fruit—such is the popular image of the native-born.

IV

Children of the Ingathering

Aharon Yadlin, Minister of Education, 1974–1977

The children of the [Jewish] immigration from Moslem countries are experiencing in the most acute form all the consequences of the meeting of different cultures as the direct result of the ingathering of the exiles. The youth who arrived with the immigration from Islamic nations after the establishment of the State were confronted with two sets of values: One was that of their parents, the other that of Israel's society at the time— values they could not easily accept. The communities in which these youngsters originated were distinguished by their traditional approach, their social structure rooted in the large family which formed the basic social unit. Israel, the absorbing country, advocated the modern Western approach and a social and economic structure which freed the individual from dependence on large family groups and was marked by its rational and individualistic ideology. If the aims defined in the State Education Law are supposed to be the declared expression of Israeli society, then they do not bear sufficient relevance to the community of new immigrants who preserve the traditional and authoritative patterns of the patriarchal family system and whose way of life has only marginally been affected by Western civilization. . . . Immigrant youth is thus faced with the danger of severance from the old values while not yet having acquired citizenship in the world of the new. In the field of cultural integration, Israeli society is confronted with the important question, Is there any justification at all for granting educational priority to the values of Western culture? . . . There can be no doubt that the processes of cultural integration will be

93

much prolonged. But these processes must be sustained without singling out any particular community and without eliminating those cultural characteristics marked by nobility of character and of Jewish spirit.
—Excerpts from an essay, "On the Character of Israeli Youth," 1970.

To be an immigrant child is never easy. To have been a young inheritor of the biblical prophecy of the ingathering of the exiles has been especially difficult.

The country to which the first of the ingathered brought their children was a malaria-infested backwater of the Ottoman Empire where hardly a plow scratched a furrow in its decaying earth. Mark Twain visited Palestine in 1867 and was taken aback. In *The Innocents Abroad* he portrayed an area of Galilee as follows:

There is not a solitary village throughout its whole extent—not for thirty miles in either direction. There are two or three small clusters of Bedouin tents, but not a single permanent habitation. One may ride ten miles, hereabouts, and not see ten human beings. To this region one of the prophecies is applied: "I will bring the land into desolation, and your enemies which dwell therein shall be astonished at it." . . . Gray lizards, those heirs of ruin, of sepulchers and desolation, glided in and out among the rocks or lay still and sunned themselves. Where prosperity has reigned and fallen; where glory has flamed and gone out; . . . where gladness was and sorrow is; where the pomp of life has been, and silence and death brood in its high places—there this reptile makes his home and mocks at human vanity.

Benjamin Disraeli, Queen Victoria's mercurial prime minister, puzzled over the riddle of Jewry's obstinate attachment to this blighted place after having been exiled from it for well-nigh two thousand years. In 1847 he published a novel called *Tancred,* and in it he predicted: "The vineyards of Israel have ceased to exist, but the Eternal Law enjoins the children of Israel to celebrate the vintage. A race that persists in celebrating their vintage although they have no fruits to gather will regain their vineyards."

Thirty-odd years later it began to happen. A band of Jews fleeing Russian pogroms trekked to the Judean Plain and founded a village which they called Rishon le-Zion, First in Zion. They planted vineyards and established wine cellars and the tidings of *aliyah* sounded.

Aliyah means "ascent, going up." By tradition, the Jew does

not migrate to the Land of Israel, he goes up; newcomers are not immigrants, they are *olim*, "ascenders." This is Bible language. Thus did the children of Israel "go up" from the land of Egypt and thus did Cyrus, King of Persia, invite the captives of the first Babylonian exile to return to Jerusalem and rebuild its temple, saying: "Whosoever there is among you of all His people—his God be with him—let him go up."

A Yemenite child and her great-great grandmother. The country still grapples with the problem of how to establish an equilibrium between the value systems of the East and the West.

The immigrant waves came from the East and the West carrying tens of thousands of children with them.

Inspired Jews in every age tried to "go up," but rarely prospered. Most succumbed to nature's perils and to the even harsher inflictions of whoever was the ruling overlord of the era. For then as today, the Promised Land lay astride strategic routes of empires, making it the object of conquest and reconquest fourteen times in almost as many centuries—by Romans, Byzantines, Arabs, Crusaders, Mamluks, Ottomans, and British. Toward the close of the nineteenth century something like twenty-five thousand Messiah-thirsting Jews persevered in Jerusalem, Hebron, Tiberias, and Safed, all of them pious, some of them outstanding scholars and most of them living off charity from abroad. Then came Rishon Le-Zion, the planting of the first vineyards, the aliyah.

What wrought the turnabout from awaiting the messianic redemption of Zion to actually initiating Zion's national revival?

In Europe old orders were toppling and the map changed and changed again under the impact of irresistible national impulses for self-determination. Caught in the turmoil, which in places swept the ghetto walls away, Jews groped for answers to their own perplexities.

Placing their trust in the promised freedoms of the new orders, some preached assimilation as the solution to their chronic homelessness. Others, men with longer memories, seized upon Judaism's messianic vision and harnessed it to the nationalist secular currents. Their vocation was the revival of Jewish statehood. An ancient Jewish nerve was tapped and what was a spiritual yearning for redemption became a national liberation movement—Zionism. From then on every anti-Semitic excess, wherever committed, impelled ever more of its victims to turn to Jerusalem, not just for prayer but for national renewal. The tide of aliyah ascended and swelled: First it was a tiny rivulet and then a stream and the stream became a river and the river a rapids. By the end of World War II more than half a million Jews had "gone up"; meanwhile, six million more died in the Nazi gas chambers.

The holocaust provoked the Jews of Palestine in a battle for freedom from British tutelage, which had all but barred Jewish entry. More than six thousand, one percent of the then Jewish population of Palestine, died in a War of Independence that reestablished a Jewish state 1,875 years after the Romans had destroyed the original. A first act of the new state was to throw open the doors of the country to every Jew who wanted to come. By law, the Law of Return, any Jew

(*Below*) They came as refugees, from the Middle East countries mostly.

(*Overleaf*) Children at the Kfar Habad youth village.

could now enter without restriction and be granted automatic citizenship. This was Israel's raison d'être—the ingathering of the exiles.

They came. From the East and the West they came carrying tens of thousands of children with them. Ships and aircraft transported virtually whole communities from Yemen and Libya and Iraq and Syria. They brought the survivors from the Nazi death camps and from the displaced persons camps; from the cities, mountains, and deserts of Morocco, Tunis, Algeria, Kurdistan, Afghanistan; the surviving remnants from Romania, Bulgaria, Yugoslavia, Poland, and Czechoslovakia. Besides the young, they brought their old, the sick, the handicapped, the illiterate, the diseased, and the deranged.

A population of 650,000 eventually welcomed 1,500,000 more. Refugees absorbed refugees. Together—those who came because they thought the Messiah had come or was coming, those who came because they had nowhere else to go, those who came to rebuild their shattered lives, and those who came because of the Zionist idea—the

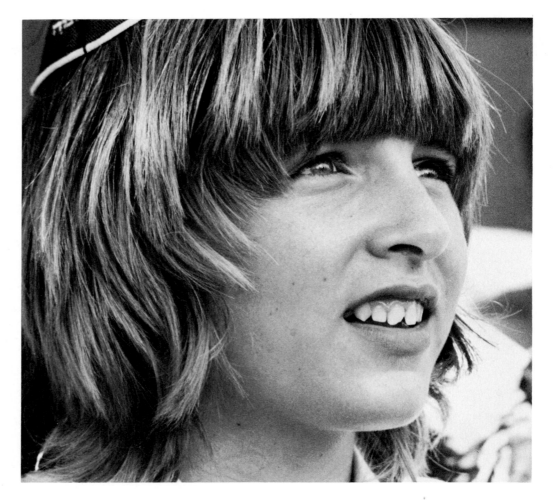

101

population of the Jewish state now came from a hundred different countries, speaking at least seventy languages. An exiled, scattered, homeless people had set out on a trail of voluntary mass self-repatriation to reestablish its sovereignty in the land of its birth—and had succeeded. Nothing like this had happened in human history before.

The script was fabulously dramatic and its plot without compare. But for many of its multitudinous cast—and for the children most of all—the roles were often trying. Speak to adults who were youngsters then, the children of that ingathering, and they will tell you of the hardships they underwent. Most lived rootless and poor, crowded into tents and huts, their fathers without jobs in a society whose ways were different and whose language most did not understand.

"To have been an immigrant child in those days," says Yoseph Abutti, "was to wake up in the morning in an overcrowded shanty and to wonder why our parents had ever brought us here. I remember old-timers visiting us to hand out candies and telling us how, when they had first arrived as children, things had been worse—as if this made our daily lives any easier."

Yoseph Abutti was fifteen then, when he came with his parents and seven brothers and sisters from Libya. He is now a Tel Aviv attorney. "My father believed, he honestly believed, that with Israel's establishment the Messiah was coming. So when Arabs in Tripoli burnt our synagogue, we came to Israel with all the rest. I'll never forget that first winter in a tent—mud and cold and meager rations; it was sheer misery. My father and two older brothers finally got jobs, road building. That first evening they came home their backs were breaking. My mother cried, my brothers and sisters cried, we all cried. We wouldn't let our father go back to that job, not for anything. You have to understand. Where we came from a Jewish father is a patriarch; he is king of the whole family. He commanded our absolute obedience and God help us if we ever disobeyed. Our father used to have a small leather shop in the *mellah,* the ghetto. He didn't earn much but he was his own master. Now, here in Israel, he was made into a common laborer—a common laborer! Over there only Arabs did that kind of work, not Jews. But my father did go back to that job. He had no choice—we had to eat. In my eyes, as a youngster, he was never the same again. He was no longer family king, not to me. I eventually joined a youth village for immigrant kids, went into the army, then was accepted into a preuniversity course to complete my matriculation. I then studied law—and here I am father of

three sabras of my own. When I think how far we've come as Israelis, I say thank God we came. But those first years—they were really tough."

Yoseph Abutti's tale of youth is the story of tens of thousands of immigrant children who were a part of that flood tide which swept Israel's shores in the aftermath of Independence. They were to be labeled children of the "other Israel." They were not like the sabras whose parents had blazed a trail to build a new society and identity, pave their own roads, construct their own towns, plant their own vineyards. These were mostly sons and daughters of scarred people, the majority penniless and skill-less, refugees to be rehabilitated and absorbed. Circumstances had made them so. Many of the youngsters were orphans, survivors of the Nazis, and the overwhelming number were children of large families from Moslem countries, societies long in decline. All had one thing in common—they were Jewish. They were Jewish, wanting to live in the new free Jewish state. But beyond that, they were as disparate as their myriad backgrounds. So many had come to the new country to be given a better life, not to become its pioneers. They were simply not equipped.

The mass ingathering happened so fast that there was really nowhere to put them all. Evacuated British army camps were commandeered, abandoned houses occupied, and tent cities hastily erected. Initially this was all the country could afford; its coffers were quite empty, there wasn't much to eat, and austerity governed everything. Immigrant youngsters had no schools to go to and no secure world outside the idleness of their own distressed families. Their consolation was that they were in a country they could call their own, surrounded by a community that welcomed them, wanted them, and shared everything they had to assist them out of their migrant traumas.

Something had to be done quickly to find long-term absorption improvisations that would improve the existing intolerable expedients. The *ma'abara* enterprise was conceived—transit districts consisting of sprawling prefabricated compounds equipped with temporary school buildings, clinics, makeshift shops, and central community services. They were really refugee camps. Relief programs on a grand scale were instituted—road building, tree planting, sewerage digging—that provided jobs of a sort. Overseas, Jewish communities mobilized material help—in America, the United Jewish

Appeal—in what was to become an unprecedented self-taxation campaign to assist the financing of permanent housing, agricultural settlement, and social welfare. Slowly, new apartment estates began to rise in the immediate vicinity of the transit districts so that, looking out of their hut windows, people could see the construction progress on their homes. Difficulties began to ease as the newcomers haltingly organized their lives and gradually took control of their own daily needs. Out of all this came new communities. As the prefabricated districts gradually gave way to permanent housing, many of the new communities began to thrive as neighborhoods of existing cities, or embryos of new development towns, or nuclei of hundreds of new cooperative farm villages.

The *ma'abara* of the 1950s and 1960s is now a hazy memory, a rather bleak one for many a youngster who grappled, as only the immigrant spirit knows how, to acquire instant citizenship in that bright world beyond the perimeter, the world of the sabras.

Youth Aliyah, which helped thousands of these children toward their goal, is unique to Israel. It is a nationwide enterprise of youth communities—villages and residential educational centers—staffed by experts and supervised by a central coordinating service agency. Its major responsibility is to rescue Jewish children from oppressed Jewish communities and bring them to Israel for rehabilitation, education, and training.

Youth Aliyah was born in the early thirties on the eve of Adolf Hitler's rise to power. It was conceived by a woman in Berlin called Recha Freier, a rabbi's wife, who, deciphering the madman's writing on the wall, urged Jewish parents to get their children, if not themselves, out of Germany quickly to Palestine before the writing became reality. Her initiative was made concrete by Henrietta Szold, originally from Baltimore, who devoted the rest of her life to these children, organizing their reception in kibbutzim and supervising their education and training. The child rescue scheme promptly became a national enterprise sponsored by the Jewish Agency, the representative body of the Jewish community in pre–World War II Palestine. Funds were allocated and emissaries dispatched to assemble the children and transport them out of Germany. The more Hitler's vise squeezed, the more feverish did the rescue mission become. Youth Aliyah spread its operations and expanded its absorption facilities, embarking on the construction of special children's villages and educational centers. By the time the Nazis had wrapped their barbed wire around the bleeding body of Europe, thousands of Jewish children had been saved. Most, however, were trapped, and of these, 1.5 million were to be systematically worked, starved, shot, and gassed to death. When the carnage ended, Youth Aliyah salvaged from the debris some tens of thousands, mainly orphans. They were cradled and carried to Israel to the children's villages and centers, there to be nurtured slowly back from the shadows of the crematoria to the land of the living. It was a long journey, an exercise in the mass rehabilitation of traumatized tortured children whose eyes were glazed by the sight of hell.

Then came the refugee flood from Arab countries, swelled by families so big as to reduce the national average age by a decade and more. Every hastily constructed tent city and *ma'abara* was whirling with children, the air full of their noises. They were in need of help—of homes the parents could not yet provide, of education the schools could not offer and of training that nobody quite knew how to devise.

So Youth Aliyah stepped forward. It could not take them all but it could do a lot. Few of its educators had experienced this new type of ward, Jewish boys and girls from North African and Asian backgrounds as varied in temperament as the climate of their geographies. Trial and error ruled as the specialists experimented with unproven educational models until they produced a program of education worthy of the name. In the process immigrant parents by

(*Opposite*) An alleyway in a desert development town.

110

From every geography and of every
hue . . .

bound to the Jewish state by the bond of faith, history, and memory.

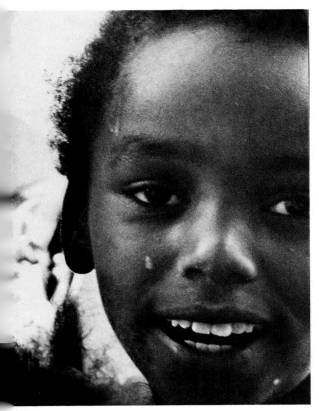

the thousands, hitherto unused to the departure of any family member from the patriarchal homestead, now entrusted their youngsters to the charge and care of Youth Aliyah. In every children's village, what began as an unruly motley of bewildered youngsters slowly evolved into a community engaged in imbibing not only a solid education and sound skills but also good citizenship.

Examine the roster of Israeli academics and professionals, political leaders and labor heads, kibbutz founders and cultural pacesetters and one finds an impressive representation of Youth Aliyah graduates, both former child survivors of the holocaust and former children of the *ma'abara*. Such is the achievement of this unusual enterprise, and its work goes on.

But what of the rest, the overwhelming majority who stayed put with their parents in the transit camps? One of Israel's first laws was that of compulsory, free education, but this was easier said than done. Given the school-age population explosion—from 150,000 in 1948 to almost 550,000 by the mid-fifties—there were just not enough schools, enough teachers, enough desks, books, anything. Everybody understood that if this heterogeneous mass of newcomers was ever to be welded into a single united nation, they had to start with the children. Only the school could give them a common language—Hebrew—and only there could the process of cultural and civic absorption begin. Thus, in the characteristic fashion of Israel's uneven progression forward, the makeshift configuration had to suffice until something better could be devised.

The first step was a crash construction program of prefabricated huts that were called schools. What identified them as such were the blackboards and the rustic desks. As for the teachers, almost anyone with a knowledge of the three Rs became a candidate for a job; and given the chronic shortage of classroom space, the children went to school in shifts. To encourage this primitive machinery, roving inspectors were appointed and volunteers and girl soldiers were mobilized. They were enough to keep the system going, but clearly this was no way to educate a nation. The government had to do something drastic and dramatic.

It did, by giving education a budgetary priority second only to that of defense. The palliative stopgaps gradually succumbed to professional programming so that with each passing year more and more of the hit-or-miss teacher apprentices were replaced by qualified personnel. Modern school structures rose as the shanty classrooms came down, and regular school hours took the place of the

erratic shift system. Teacher incentives improved, so that by the mid-sixties the nation's school system had caught up with itself. A people steeped in a heritage of learning could now begin to reach out for excellence.

Dina Azulai, a retired elementary school principal who began her profession in a school hut and went every step of the way from improvisation to specialization, recalls the early years: "For all the frustrations, there was challenge. We had little more to give than our willpower and that was often taxed beyond limit. I had been to high school in Casablanca and knew some Hebrew, so I was able to pass as a qualified teacher. But imagine standing before a group of

Israel is a country where many a parent learns Hebrew from the children.

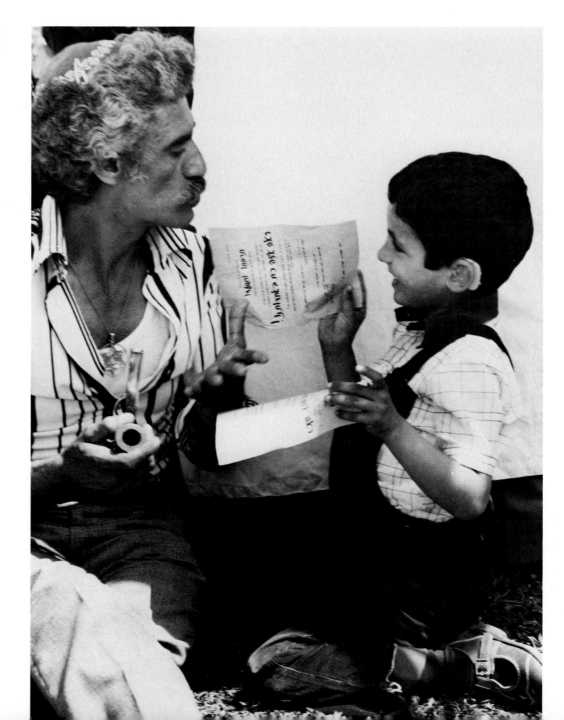

forty children and more—all crammed into a hut room, children from Iraq and Libya and Egypt and Kurdistan, with some from Romania and Poland, and saying: 'Right, let's begin to be Israelis!' Songs—oh how grateful I was for every Hebrew song I ever learned! Whenever I got stumped and didn't know what to say next, what to do next, I'd start the kids singing. That's how they learned Hebrew—through songs and games. And once they had the language, they began learning. What a satisfaction that was, to watch the crowd become a group of curious-minded schoolkids. Never mind the primitive conditions. Walls don't make schools; people do, and we were a devoted lot of amateurs. We didn't know much but we had energy, spirit. We were

and seeing through the touch of hands.

motivated. Perhaps it was the fact that for many of the kids secular studies were a new experience, perhaps it was the extra drive immigrant children generally show, perhaps it was the extra challenge we teachers faced, perhaps it was the adventure of the new country—whatever it was, and for all the enormous mistakes we made, we opened those kids' minds. That's education!''

True, it was not the most orthodox, and certainly not the most satisfactory, mode of tuition a child might enjoy, but it was evidently sufficient to carry the majority, albeit haltingly, grade by grade, through elementary school into high school, vocational school, or night school, and ultimately, in the case of many, into a university. What the immigrant teen-agers failed to acquire in the classrooms

A student at Boys Town vocational school in Jerusalem.

118

Within a relatively short period vocational schools sprouted throughout the country, many of them catering to young immigrants.

they eventually obtained in the army. In fact, the army became an indispensable finishing school for immigrant teen-agers, teaching them language, textbook knowledge, and civic values. These were years when many a recruit spent as much time in the classroom as on the firing range.

Thus did the children of the ingathering progressively enter the mainstream of Israeli life, moving up the educational ladder until equipped and confident enough to begin competing for their own place outside.

Most of today's sabras, perhaps close to sixty percent, are the children of those who were the children of the ingathering. Hebrew is their mother tongue and their ways are Israeli. But there is a dif-

(*Overleaf*) Parents and youngsters join in reviving folk ceremonies that were all but forgotten.

ference. They move between two cultural worlds—the Western and the Oriental. For some this is accomplished with natural ease and for others it creates conflict.

There are parents and educators who look back with anger upon those years in the school huts, not because of the deprivation that reigned but because of the presumption that ruled. Those responsible for the schools, the state educational authorities, were mainly of European (Ashkenazic) origin; the pupils were mostly Oriental (Sephardic). Too many teachers were too quick in grafting their Western ways onto the Sephardic youngsters, without being sufficiently attentive and sensitive to their pride of origin and community identity. Most of the children were products of a tradition—social, cultural, and religious—whose roots lay in the life-styles of the Mid-

Mother and daughters in
Yemenite dance.

dle Eastern and North African societies from which they had come.
Their households were extended families governed by fathers who
were patriarchs. Their schools taught obedience not individualism,
piety not rationalism.

Israel's twin government school system, the secular and the religious, fought a battle for the "souls" of these children as immigrant
parents looked on not quite understanding what the battle was about.
Most assumed that in the Jewish state all schools were religious. In
the end it was the secular system that won the highest registration.
It took a few years and a government crisis before parental freedom
of choice could be exercised without restraint.

Both systems, the secular and the religious, had their roots in
the Ashkenazi-dominated pre-State community and both set about,

Faces mirror places of myriad migrant waves.

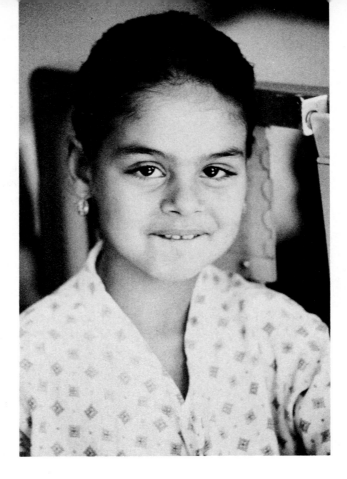

Classic faces of Sephardi
children.

wittingly or not, to "Israelify" the youngsters in their own image.
What was once called in America the melting pot became in Israel the
pressure cooker. Hardly had the immigrant youngsters mastered Hebrew when they were put through what amounted, in many a classroom, to a course in de-Sephardization. The goal was to acculturate
the pupils as fast as possible. The youngsters, particularly teen-agers,
were often willing collaborators, for to them this was the route to the
sabra world outside. The result was that many hastily jettisoned the
traditions and customs of their parents in favor of what was, too
often, a Western veneer, no more. These youngsters would return
daily from school to their tradition-bound homes, to fathers striving
hard to hold on to their patriarchal authority, loyal to the tribal wisdoms and educated in simple crafts hardly relevant to the country's
immediate needs. Here, if anything, was a prescription for a massive
generation gap. The cemented, secure value system of the large family structure with its tried and tested traditions began to crack. As it
did so, people in authority began to wonder whether the ethnocentric
Ashkenazic way, dominated by the educational principles of the nation's founders, was indeed legitimate. Aharon Yadlin, a veteran kibbutz member, who was to become minister of education, was indeed
right to put the question, "Is there any justification at all for granting
educational priority to the values of Western culture?"

Out of that question, posed in 1970, came a measure of re-thinking that persists to this day. The nation's school enterprise is still seized with the problem of how to establish an educational equilibrium between the value systems of the East and the West, a synthesis of the best of the Jewish cultures, the Sephardic and the Ashkenazic. Clearly, this is a long, integrative process which time alone will crystallize into a homogeneous medium, just as the nation itself is still integrating its component parts into a cultural whole. No wonder, then, that many youngsters from Oriental homes remain suspended between the two worlds, the East and the West, tending toward the Ashkenazic at school and the Sephardic at home.

But something important has begun to happen. These sabras are now bent upon the search for their own identity as never before and the school curricula are gradually bending with them. This is not the aggressive digging for "roots" characteristic of American society; rather it is an awakening of an intrinsic integrity as a cultural community which carried into Israel much that was archaic but also much

Hebrew-speaking children from Vietnam are a part of the Ben Gurion University, Beersheba, youth program. They and their parents were rescued as "boat people."

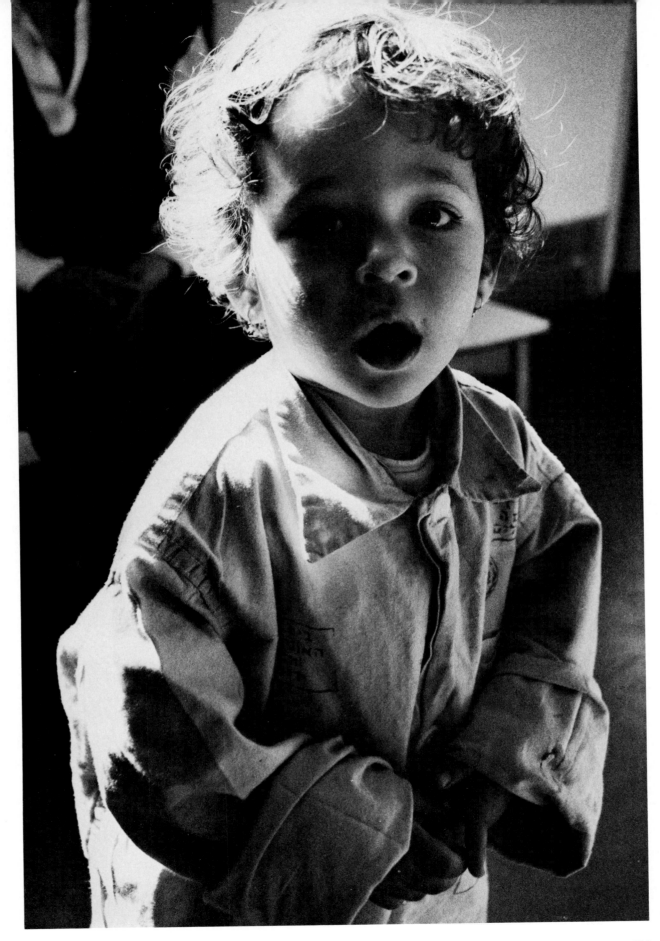

that was beautiful. It is that which was beautiful to which the youngsters are coming alive. Thus, across the country, young people from Moroccan homes and Yemenite homes, from Indian, Iraqi, and Syrian homes, are joining with their elders in reviving family traditions and community festivals that brought so much richness to their lives in the countries of their dispersion. The distinctive customs are all now touched and colored by the equally distinctive Israeli quality which the young naturally introduce. But the songs are the old ones, the dances are the same, and so is much of the dress and the food. Grandparents and grandchildren often reach across to each other, helping to heal a gap of culture that inflicted itself upon the generation in between. This is a leavening, a cultural continuity by osmosis, a natural self-editing of community identities. Nothing has enriched Israel's folklore and heritage more than the increasingly confident revival of colorful traditions as varied as the origins of this nation. It is proof that Israel is finally maturing out of its migrant mentality as its first generation of Sephardic sabras, the children of the children of the ingathering, graduate into society carrying with them their own pride and style. With each passing year they achieve growing prominence in government, in the army, in science, in the arts, everywhere.

Some, however, just can't make it. They remain the "other Israel," vividly identifiable still as the Israel of the underprivileged and the poor. Many of their parents had themselves arrived in the country as youngsters but had failed to scale the ladder beyond the *ma'abara* schools. They had moved in space from one geography to another but had never crossed the threshold of time from the environment of their past to the advanced society of their present. So they remained trapped and their children have inherited their disadvantage. They are the nation's residual unabsorbed, invariably parents of large families. To listen to their youngsters talk is to hear the voice of the sabras of the slums:

The scene is Acre, a winter's night. It is raining. Boys and girls are hanging noisily around in the local community club, playing cards, watching television, trying their hand at Ping-Pong. Most have long hair, wear blue jeans, and are of Oriental origin. Their parents came from Arab countries in 1948 or shortly thereafter. They themselves were born in Israel, sabras in name but not in prototype. Some go to school, others don't, and some are known to the police. This is where they congregate, the club. Their homes are plaster-peeling overcrowded tenements where every living room doubles as a bed-

room. The club is the one place in town where they can find their own company. They are exhibitionists, egocentric and sensitive. They seek attention, enjoy an occasional scrap, and are eager to be photographed and interviewed.

"Sure," says Dudu, a lithe, lean Afro-haired sixteen-year old who wears pants as tight as his skin, "sure I'm going to get a job, but not the one the employment exchange sent me to last month, a shoe factory. It was a miserable dump. I'd rather stick around here and have fun with my pals. Whenever I go a bit short, I put in a few hours at the building site; a few of us do that to keep us going. I once

tried going to the vocational school but I gave up after a couple of months. I couldn't get the arithmetic into my head." Dudu takes out a cigarette and lights up, cupping the flame ceremoniously. "There are ten of us at home; two of my brothers are doing army service. I guess I'll stick around till I'm called up. They tell me the army will try to teach me something, that it will teach a trade to kids like us. If not, I'll get out of it somehow. I'll go abroad. Why should I get myself killed for this country? What's it ever done for me?"

Mazal is also sixteen. Her taut T-shirt declares in bold red print, Miami Beach—Sunshine Paradise, a gift from a visiting tourist

via the local social worker. Mazal is dark, her hair up, and her eyes flash intelligently as she talks. "In our apartment nine of us live in two and a half rooms. I've never known it to be different. Yes, I still go to school but I wonder, sometimes, what's the point. Homework is a misery because I've nowhere to do it. My father was about my age when he came with his parents to Israel from Morocco in the early fifties. He never had a chance. He was a dropout from the start. He still doesn't know Hebrew properly. All his life he's been a day laborer. He'd kill me if I ever left school. 'Don't you be just a house-

wife and a cleaner like your mother,' he says. 'Learn something and marry somebody decent.' That's how he talks. He made my brothers go to vocational school or get jobs as apprentices. They're doing okay now. We kids are his self-respect. Our social worker is keen that I try for nursing. I might just do that if only I had some decent privacy and less chores at home to do. My mother goes out most evenings. She's a cleaner at the town hall and that leaves me to feed my dad and the kids. I come here to the club just to get away from it all."

The social worker is Rina, herself from a large Moroccan family who came from Casablanca in 1950. She is a graduate of Haifa University and has been working with the Acre kids for a number of years. "There must be some thirty thousand such families in Israel who never really got out of the *ma'abara,*" she explains. "We have to do something about their children and that's why I chose social work. I know them and can talk to them and they trust me. I'm one of them." In her mid-twenties, Rina talks vivaciously with an infectious sabra energy. "These are good kids," she insists. "We have to give them the chance, the opportunity to make a go of it. Some think they're discriminated against because they're Orientals, Sephardim. That's stupid. Obviously they have it tougher than most Ashkenazic kids because their parents began lower down the scale when they first arrived. Most Europeans, the Ashkenazim, had some grounding in modern education and could climb the ladder quicker. We have to break the poverty cycle and to do that we have to change the whole environment. Change that and the children will change. That's why I put so much faith in Project Renewal. It's a fantastic idea. If only it works it could offer a whole new beginning for so many of these kids—and their parents as well."

Project Renewal is a bold countrywide enterprise. Begun in 1979, it has as its objective the renewal of the immigrant neighborhoods hurriedly constructed in the 1950s and which by the 1960s had sunk into slums. What gives Project Renewal its unique dimension is its comprehensive concept. The idea is to replan and rebuild each slum neighborhood around professionally staffed community facilities and services so as to help lift the residents not only out of their physical disadvantage but also out of their slum mentality; in short, to eradicate the "other Israel." The emphasis is on the youth and on the family, not just on buildings; to engage the neighborhood dwellers in every phase of the development and in the determination of their own community priorities. Just as their original neighborhoods were built with the voluntary aid of Jewish communities overseas, so is Project Renewal the product of their active assistance and planning involvement. Larger Jewish communities abroad have "adopted" as their own specific slum areas earmarked for renewal in partnership with the government and the respective municipalities.

Says Rina: "It's going to take years to do it but the start is already having its effect. It is giving people for the first time a sense of worth, and that means pride. What I and those I work with are trying to do now is first of all to get new community services really going, like the youth club, so that what the kids can't get in their homes, the community will provide. We're on the right track. These youngsters deserve a better deal and we've got to give it to them. If we don't, it's going to be a big scab on the face of Israel's future."

Rina is right. The rehabilitation of this youth represents a primary, indeed the supreme, domestic challenge. Numerically they represent a significant segment of the population, enough to leave its mark on the quality of life and inner stamina of the nation. Israel can tolerate such neglect only at its own peril. The Jewish state has few natural resources (it has no oil at all). By its very smallness it will always have to make up in quality what it lacks in quantity. Thus education has always been the first priority after defense. Project Renewal represents the climax of an exhaustive investment in the nation's youth, from prekindergarten projects to free elementary, junior, and high schools, to expanded vocational schools, to preacademic university programs, to parental-guidance courses, to army-sponsored educational programs, and more. From start to finish, each of these investments has been geared to the needs of the weaker sectors of the population, the children from disadvantaged homes, and the effort has been repaid a thousandfold in the new sabra currency. Now ahead stretches the last and toughest hill—the climb into Israel of the "other Israel," the unabsorbed residue of that mass ingathering a generation and more ago. This is what Project Renewal is setting out to do.

Meanwhile, though in far smaller numbers than before, the current of the migration tide rolls on. Its major flow in recent years—and it was a dramatic one—is Jews from the Soviet Union. Over 150,000 arrived since the exodus from Russia began in the early 1970s, only to again be reduced to a trickle by the early 1980s.

Its children often tell of high drama as they recount the tale of their personal exodus. Listen to Nicolai, fourteen years old, formerly of Leningrad and now of Ashdod. One year after he, his parents, and his younger brother Yuri reached Israel, this is what he says: "In

On the doorstep of the Zion orphanage, Jerusalem—brothers who had arrived that day from Russia.

Leningrad me and my brother were like everybody else. We had friends, and went to school and twice a week I went to the academy to learn violin. My teacher, Kutzinov—good old Kutzinov—looked just like a Russian count. That's what we called him—the Count. One day I came home from school and I felt something was wrong, different. Father was home. He is an engineer and he never came home before suppertime. He said he had come early because something special had happened. He had just been given permission to go to Israel; all of us were going to Israel. He and mother looked so excited and happy. I couldn't understand why. Why Israel? They had never said anything about it before. Only Jews went to Israel. I didn't even know where it was. And then father told us that we were Jews. He told us we were Jews, all of us. He told us that mother's grandfather had even been a rabbi and that he hadn't told us before because of school and the neighbors and the teachers. They might not have liked it, he said. I remember feeling funny inside and Yuri—he's my younger brother—cried." At this point Nicolai takes a deep breath

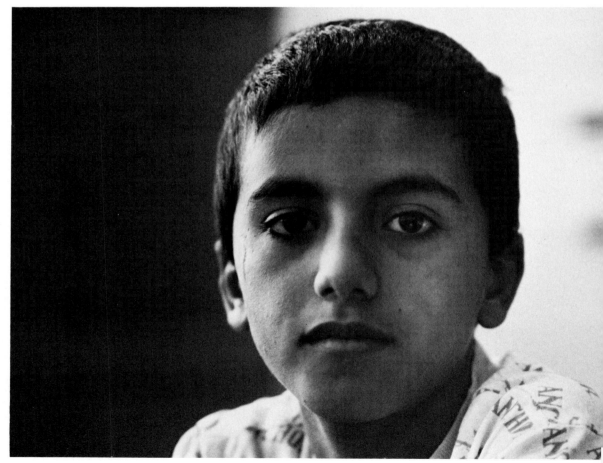

The "new immigrant" look: children at an absorption center for new arrivals from the Soviet Union.

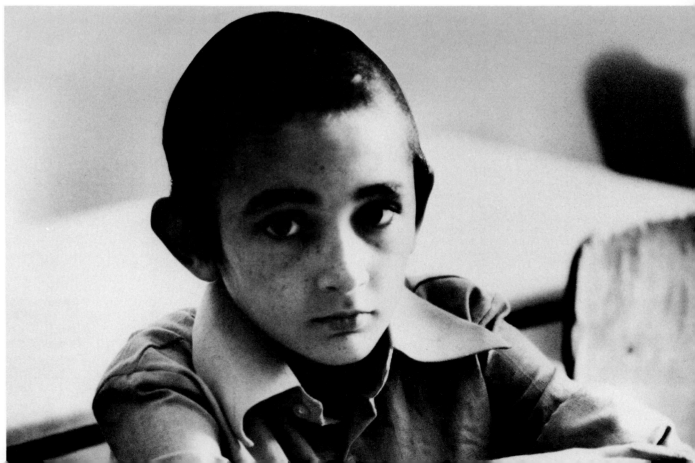

and his dark eyes blink as though still digesting this momentous truth, the truth that changed his world. He sits on the steps of the three-story apartment house in Ashdod, where many families from Russia live. Pensively, he cups his face in his hands. They are as light and as fragile-looking as his whole frame. His long fingers caress his chin as they would the strings of a violin. Nicolai goes on: "Next day I told the Count. I told him we were going to Israel. I just had to because I like him and trust him. He looked at me so strangely. He put down his violin, closed his eyes, and then tears ran down his cheeks. I went up to him and he hugged me. 'You are Jewish?' he

From Moscow to Mevaseret, an absorption center on the outskirts of Jerusalem.

142

asked. I nodded. I was too confused to speak. 'I'm a Jew too,' he said. I was so surprised I almost choked. My mind was in a whirl. Think of it, the Count a Jew and I hadn't known and I was a Jew and I hadn't known and now he was staying and we were going. He gave me another hug and asked me to leave him alone. The last I saw was him sitting there alone in the rehearsal room. A few months ago I wrote the Count a letter telling him about how I was still learning violin in Israel. One sentence I wrote in Hebrew just to show I'm learning it in school—it's terribly hard. Then, the other day, he sent me his reply—all in Hebrew. A whole letter all in Hebrew from the Count. And do you know what? I couldn't understand a word of it. The writing was clear, almost as if each letter was drawn with a pen, but the words were beyond me. So I showed it to my teacher, and do you know what she said? She said it's written in the old-fashioned Hebrew, the Hebrew they wrote the Bible in and which nobody uses anymore, only scholars. The Count, a Hebrew scholar! Who would believe that in Leningrad? He kept it a secret all these years. I wonder if they'll ever let him out."

Encapsuled in Nicolai's story is the tragedy and the triumph of a whole community, three million strong, which was severed from the Jewish world for well over half a century and which the Communist system had condemned to spiritual death. But most Jews simply would not let their faith perish, despite the outlawing of Jewish schools, of Jewish cultural life, of the study of Hebrew, of Zionism. Emboldened by Israel's amazing victory of the Six Day War in 1967, Russian Jews in the tens of thousands dared defy the regime and demand the right to emigrate to Israel. Led by men and women who were ready to risk the worst—and some languish still in Siberian jails—they called for, and they asked, Western public opinion to support, not counterrevolution but "repatriation." This was their slogan, the right to be repatriated to their families, their homeland. Every nationality had its homeland: the Ukrainians, Ukraine, the Lithuanians, Lithuania, the Georgians, Georgia, and the Jews, Israel. This was their moral claim and they voiced it with a display of courage that captured the imagination and the heart of much of the free world. By the early seventies, the Russian door began to open, not wide, not freely, but enough for Jews in the thousands to begin to move through. Most of the measured, restricted, controlled exodus has reached Israel and, given the imponderables of Russian behavior, nobody can foretell what future lies in store for those who wish to leave but have not yet been permitted to go.

Ask the young immigrants from Russia what they find the strangest thing about the Jewish state and as likely as not they'll say: the fact that nobody forces you to do anything. This, above all—the freedom—is what initially staggers the children and elders alike. It is bewildering for children to hear their parents at home grappling with what are often for them dilemmas of choice, never having experienced freedom of choice before. There, in that other world from which they have come, one is given a job, told where to work and where to live. To go out and decide for oneself what employment one wants and then compete with the next person for it—this takes some getting used to.

"I remember those first weeks after we arrived in the absorption center," says Moshe (he was Mischa in Moscow). "My father nearly burst a blood vessel every time he read a newspaper. He simply couldn't believe that correspondents would dare write the things they did about official policy." Now a sixteen-year-old lanky adolescent, Moshe speaks with an almost sabra Hebrew that testifies to the four years his family has been in Israel. Only his light complexion betrays his northern origin. "In our school in Tel Aviv there must be at least about fifty kids from Russia, some from the European and some from the Asian part. Most of us by now speak Hebrew together. There are special additional Russian-language classes for the new kids who come. It was difficult at first and I think what all of us found

hardest to adjust to was the discipline—or what we thought was the lack of it. We just weren't used to the freedom, to the open discussions with the teachers, to the informality of everything. At home, me and my parents and my older sister and brother—we used to discuss very seriously how we should handle ourselves. Now we laugh about it. And we laugh about something else as well. In Russia, people used to call us Jews. In the Jewish state we're called Russians. That really is very funny."

Israelis are that way. After all, most people arrived sometime from some place, speaking some language. The immigrant youngsters never really escape their identity, the fact that at one time in their life they were children of the ingathering.

Immigrant families from Arab countries are invariably large and are given the title "bru-khot yeladim"—blessed with many offspring.

V

Youth of Utopia

Shoshana, Aged Sixteen, Kibbutz Yagur, the Z'vulun Valley

I think—as far as I'm concerned anyway—that being a kibbutznik is something rather special. The kibbutz is the only place I'd want to be. I don't say we're better than the kids outside but we're certainly different. I see it every time I'm with them, with kids from town—on youth movement hikes or at camp, places like that. We kibbutz kids tend to do things in our own way. We think differently; that's how we're brought up—to pull together. Town kids say we're better off than they are, that we have all kinds of opportunities they don't have because of our own separate youth community. I suppose we are better off—in some ways more independent. But I can't really judge because I've never lived in a town. Whenever we've discussed these things together and we've asked the kids from Tel Aviv or Haifa or Jerusalem, Okay, if you think kibbutz is better, why don't you decide to live on a kibbutz? Most say no. They say they wouldn't want to spend their whole lives in the communal way of living. They say it's too narrow, too restricting. Well, I think they're wrong. The kibbutz today isn't what it used to be. When I think what Yagur is like today and compare it with the stories our grandparents tell us of what it used to be like, I honestly believe we're not narrow at all, as people I mean. In the old days everything had to be very ideological and disciplined and everybody had to live exactly the same way. They had to because they were building a totally new way of life in the middle of one big swamp; things were tough and dangerous. Look at Yagur now; it's almost a town. That's something to be proud of, to be born in a place like this

149

which your own grandparents and parents created out of nothing. Sure, we still live by kibbutz principles and I think we youngsters have the best of both worlds: We have our own **chevra**, *our own youth community, just as in the old days, and we also have the advantages of a developed kibbutz. There's so much going on here and to do here and, if we want to, we can even go on to higher studies after the army. I agree kibbutz isn't for everybody, but I also bet there are people in town who would be better off as people in kibbutz. I also suppose, for that matter, that there are some kibbutzniks who'd be better off in town. I think to live in kibbutz happily you either have to be born in one or have the right kind of temperament. Those who don't probably leave soon enough.*

The word *kibbutz* is probably best translated as "togetherness"—the notion of community in its highest sense. Its origins lie in a swampy shoreline on the southern tip of the Sea of Galilee, where, in 1909, a tiny group of young pioneers put together a ramshackle commune they named Degania—God's Grain. They could not have known then that they were beginning a social adventure that would mature into what is today a countrywide movement numbering almost three hundred kibbutz villages with a population of more than one hundred thousand. Four percent of Israelis are kibbutzniks.

When four percent of a nation accounts for a disproportionately

To be a kibbutz youngster is to enjoy a childhood that is, surely, the closest thing to utopia.

high percentage of national leadership, some fifteen percent of the gross national product, and almost sixteen percent of the volunteer officer corps—this says something, surely, for the elitist personality of kibbutz society and the kind of youngsters it breeds. Close to twenty percent of Israel's military graves are inscribed with the names of kibbutz lads.

The kibbutz has long ceased to be a mere experiment. Well into the fourth generation, it emerges as the oldest and most expansive exercise in comprehensive communal living ever attempted anywhere. Whatever its future adaptation and evolution, it is safe to predict that ten, twenty, and fifty years hence the kibbutz village pattern will, in one form or another, continue to dot Israel's landscape from northern Galilee to the southern Negev.

As is true of all great and lasting social ideas, the kibbutz ideology persevered because it grew out of a sound marriage between reality and vision cemented in a contract of compelling necessity. The necessity emanated from the incredible hardships the young Degania enthusiasts had to confront in 1909. Had they, on that marshy, malarial Sea of Galilee shoreline, not clung together, they would not have survived. Individually, they would have fled or perished because their means were meager, their farming knowledge abysmal, the environment forbidding, and the Arab marauders a menace. Settling along in isolated farmsteads, they would—as had many of their predecessors—have fallen prey one by one to the natural hazards, casualties of their own inexperience and the roaming armed bands. So they united, reinforced each other, and together worked the virgin land.

Degania would have remained a stockade of pioneer necessity had not its confines been overleaped by the energy of the moral idea it housed. It was this above all, the mission, that transformed the individuals into innovators and the compound into a kibbutz. Degania's mission was to establish a utopia—a new, rejuvenated Jewish society that would be virtuous and equal. To do this Degania turned itself into a microcosm of what its members envisaged the future society would be—one in which everyone would enjoy total equality, all would be responsible for the others, all would work together in accordance with their ability and receive according to their needs, all would share whatever they possessed and join in directly determining the will of the community. This handful of Degania idealists even shared their clothes and banned money. Who needed money within an absolutely just society where everyone in unison assumed respon-

(Opposite) Education toward work is an intrinsic part of the whole kibbutz educational system.

(Overleaf) Kibbutz youngsters are considered natural officer material. No other sector of the population furnishes the Israel Defense Forces with such a high percentage of officers.

sibility for production, shared all means of sustenance, provided every service, and where a regularly rotated elected council saw to all marketing and purchasing, reinvesting whatever profits there were back into the community?

This was infinite togetherness and it was there, by the Sea of Galilee, that Tolstoian romanticism, socialist equality, and Zionist self-redemption fused into a unique ethic of voluntary collective living bonded by a soaring idealistic fervor. The experiment was destined to attract hundreds and then thousands of like-minded volunteers, young men and women who went out to found their own fledgling communal villages. These were not eccentrics escaping into impossible dreams, nor were their ascetic settlements separatist enclaves of a sectarian cult. They were the pacesetters of the pre-State self-determination movement motivated by the conviction that building freedom and building oneself must go hand in hand. They were

Descendants of Israel's first kibbutz, Degania.

pathfinders, not peasants. So they subordinated their every energy to the discipline of the elected representative central authorities of the Jewish state-in-the-making. They did not choose advantageous sites for their adventure; they built the kibbutzim where they were told they were most needed and wherever land was to be had—in the swamps, on the rugged mountain heights, in the desert, along the frontiers, in the most improbable regions. Only the kibbutz way of life with its attendant disciplines, its willing self-sacrifice, and its exuberant spirit could have faced and tamed those wasted wilds. And only the kibbutzniks could have served as the vanguard of the return to the soil, "to build and to be built," as their popular song went.

Inevitably, from this astonishing reservoir of zeal came forth leadership and direction for a nation of exiles struggling to scratch out for themselves their own niche under the sun. Kibbutzniks (Golda Meir for one) entered the political and labor bodies then being founded. They established their own schools and youth movements. They launched cultural trends and ventures. When the time came, they volunteered for hazardous duties with the Allied forces including lone parachute missions into Nazi-occupied Europe. After the war they led the establishment of refugee escape routes out of Europe to beat the British blockade. The kibbutzim became the backbone of the secret bases of the Jewish underground, and as the battle lines for Independence were drawn, they provided many of the crack units and officers. The war over and the armistice signed, it was mainly the location of the kibbutzim, their flags planted and protected in the far-off waste places, that shaped the map of the newly founded state.

After Independence, two things happened: Among the hundreds of thousands of refugee immigrants who flooded the new Israel, some thousands—including young survivors of the Nazi holocaust—organized themselves into kibbutz groups to settle hitherto inaccessible barren tracts; and the older kibbutzim began to consolidate and invest in themselves.

Travel today through recently settled border areas and you will still come across new kibbutz villages that retain their movielike, dusty, bare stockade image, not dissimilar to the scenes in the fading photos of the old pioneer era. But stop at a veteran kibbutz of the 1980s and you enter a setting that is flourishing scenery. Except perhaps for a museum glen, nothing at all is left of the huts and the trenches, the wagons and the mules, the mosquito nets and the latrines. The old-timer who might chance by will be happy to escort you across manicured park-size lawns to the spot where the original tents had been pitched, the site of the old wooden stables and the plot that had served as the first vegetable patch. Kibbutz elders like to reminisce, not least to the visitor and most of all to their own grandchildren. And the little grandchildren revel in the heroics of the legends of their forebears.

"My saba [grandfather] says that our kibbutz is famous. He says everybody knows about it because of the way it was built. It was built in one night." Thus says Galya, an eight-year-old child of Kibbutz Hanita as she breathlessly recounts her grandfather's adventure on that night in Galilee more than forty years ago when he joined in erecting a watchtower and stockade close to the Lebanese frontier. Galya's eyes expand with the excitement of her own narration. "Saba told me how they did it. They were frightened they would be attacked so do you know what they did? They built a big tower and a high wall, all on that first night before the Arabs could discover them. And then in the morning they were attacked but saba and the others were safe inside. My saba tells me lots of stories like that of how Hanita first began. Do you know that in the beginning all this you see—those trees, the houses, the fields, everything—were rocks and stones? Saba says that for years he hardly did anything else but pick stones. He used to come home at night all bent up from clearing away rocks and stones to make the fields. Look at them now, the fields." Galya points to the undulating expanse of Hanita's tilled countryside, her tanned, dimpled face peering into the Galilee sun, her forehead knitted as though wrestling with a picture she cannot fully comprehend—of bent backs, bleak hillsides, and threatening gunmen creeping between the rocks. Thus, as the founder generation ages into retirement the newest generation picks up its tales, embellishes them, and composes them into fables.

To be born and to grow up in such surroundings is to enjoy a childhood that is, surely, the closest thing to utopia. For if, indeed, the kibbutz is practically the last word in togetherness, it follows that to be its child is to experience the ultimate in belonging and security. When kibbutz youngsters roll out of bed in the morning, they open their eyes on a world that recognizes no dichotomies. Everything about them is an extension of something else—roommates, the home, the school, the adults, the parents, the teachers, the cows, the fields, the playground, the tractors, the factory—everything belongs to them and they to it. All are occupied with the whole, dedicated to the whole, and within this whole the children come first. They are, in the

(*Below*) The enemy tank that was stopped at the kibbutz gates in the war of 1948. In those early years the geographic location of the settlements largely shaped the map of the new state.

(*Overleaf*) Kibbutz educators take pride in a collective system they claim encourages individual self-expression: a homemade puppet show with contemporary political characters.

words of one kibbutz expert, "our children." They live in an all-embracing world in which everybody and everything resides in harmonious proximity. This, at least, is what the kibbutz aspires to be.

"I remember as a child," recalls Zvi, a field crop specialist in

Veteran kibbutzim have grown into dynamic economic entities, and the extended home of the kibbutz youngster is invariably a conglomerate of farm and factory.

his early twenties, of Lavi, a religious kibbutz overlooking the Nazareth–Tiberias highway, "I remember thinking to myself that God must be a kibbutznik. Nothing can compare to a kibbutz child's life. Home was not just my parents' house, it was everywhere. The older I got, the less certain I became, of course, about the divine right of the kibbutz and by the time I entered the army, I had my doubts whether I would stay a kibbutznik at all. In fact, I left for a while."

And what brought him back?

"Two things—Lavi is home; these are my people. The kids I grew up with are almost like brothers and sisters to me. And then, I wanted my children to grow up here, to have what I had. Town life offers nothing like it and so I came back."

What about kibbutz ideology, did that have nothing to do with the decision?

"Hardly. I don't think all that many of us born into kibbutz life are great ideologues. What ties us are the roots more than the beliefs. Somewhere along the line you make your own calculation, advantages against disadvantages, and as often as not the emotional bond to the place and the family is the deciding factor that makes you want to stay. No doubt, the economic security kibbutz provides is also a consideration for some."

Indeed, it is. The veteran kibbutzim have grown into dynamic economic entities affording their members not personal affluence, but creature and cultural comforts that can be impressive, such as recre-

Taking a turn at kitchen chores. For many of the youngsters the kibbutz is home, not an instrument for social revolution as the founders conceived it.

The children's communities have their own little farms that the children work collectively under the guidance of counselors.

ation facilities that would do justice to many a country club, theater halls for homemade and outside productions, well-stocked libraries, occasional foreign travel, and functional cottage homes or apartments tastefully furnished and ringed by lawns and floral gardens.

The extended home of the modern kibbutz child is invariably

a conglomerate of farm and factory administered by the most advanced techniques of management and technology. The classic collective institutions remain intact giving substance to the sacrosanct principles of a classless and moneyless society, of common ownership and direct democracy. The inherent understanding still prevails that one works according to ability and receives according to need and that the community has the responsibility to give of itself for the national good. As at the beginning, so today, the hallmark of the kibbutz is the communal dining hall and the hub of the youngsters' lives remains the autonomous children's community. Whatever the variants, a village in Israel that does not have a central dining hall and an all-embracing, autonomous children's community cannot claim to call itself a kibbutz. It might be an offshoot of it, but it is not a kibbutz.

The children's community is special. It is equipped with every facility to enable the youngsters, as they grow up, to pursue their own group development and to gradually administer themselves as a miniature kibbutz, guided by their teachers and counselors. From birth almost, the children usually live, eat, sleep, and once they are old enough, study and work together in their own houses, set apart in their own grounds, divided according to age groups. Many of the children's communities have their own little farms and it is not uncommon to come across six-year-old first-graders tending their own sheep and chickens and planting their own field, free to dispose of the income from the produce as they see fit by the democratic vote of the group for the benefit of all. Thus, the Hanukkah decorations in

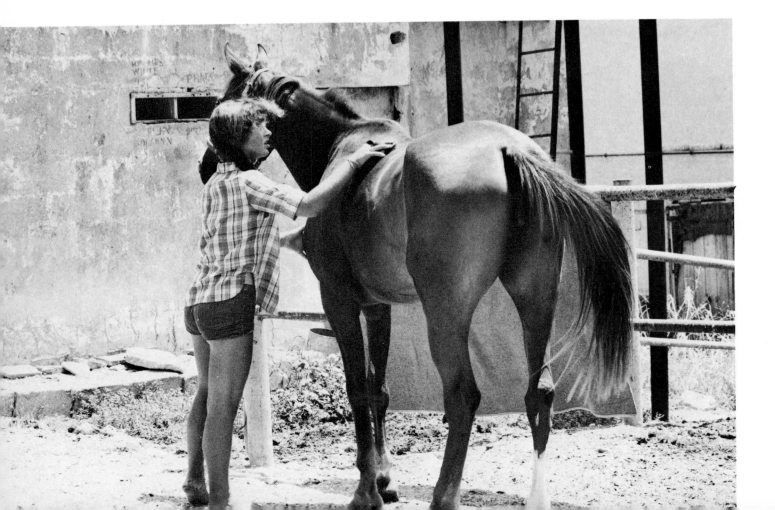

the children's dining hall or the newest game equipment may well have been acquired with the funds earned from their collective labors.

Education toward work and self-labor as human values is an intrinsic part of the whole educational system. So, too, is the indoctrination in community commitment and mutual help. Most kibbutz villages administer their own elementary schools but only a few have enough teen-agers of their own to warrant a separate high school. The latter are often established on a regional basis catering to youngsters from a number of kibbutzim of the same ideological bent, be it secular or religious, radical left, middle left, or moderate socialist. Curricula are always comprehensive and, education being the single highest community responsibility, no expense is spared in the quest for quality.

From the day the first kibbutz children's community was established, outsiders have asked, What kind of a family relationship does such a system produce when parents and youngsters have so little time together? Surely this is unnatural, unhealthy, subjecting mothers to maternal deprivation and the children to emotional dependence on the community group rather than on their natural families.

The founding matrons of kibbutz society were, by and large, a sturdy lot, not given to petit bourgeois feminine finesse. As far as they were concerned, the kibbutz was the answer to every female frustration. Here, in a society where everything was shared, where people ate together, worked together, and where children were brought up together, the woman could come into her own as a productive human being free to give expression to her own full potential. This was the creed. No longer was she a slave to fashion or to domestic chores. Any job a man could do so could she. They called this equality of sex, not women's liberation, but it amounted to the same thing. In some of the early kibbutzim people even went so far as to question the institutions of marriage and family as being obsolete relics of their bourgeois past. But then, babies began to be born and the nonsense stopped.

To release wives and mothers from kitchen and cradle, a paramount role was assigned to the communal dining hall and to the children's community. Most women could now, supposedly, work in the fields alongside the men and, generally, fully share in the running of their society. But over the years most women gradually tended to gravitate back from the fields to the community services, assuming responsibility for the running of the community kitchen and dining hall, the children's nurseries, the laundry, and the other traditionally oriented female chores. Nevertheless, it remains true today that the kibbutz life-style does permit female members a larger measure of freedom from homebound responsibilities than in the case of most average housewives outside.

"No, I don't think we have much in common with those early kibbutz matriarchs," says Nitza of Kibbutz Ein Harod, smilingly. "They probably would not like our Sabbath stylish dress and our after-work makeup. This kind of thing was taboo to them."

Nitza is the mother of three, two girls and a boy, ranging in age from eleven to two. She sits in an armchair in her attractively furnished, book-lined cottage home, her day's work done. Two of her children are playing outside and the youngest sits on her lap leafing through a picture book. It is the most relaxed interlude of the kibbutz day, those couple of hours between work's end and suppertime, after which the children will be escorted to bed in their dorms.

Says Nitza: "I can understand those who think the kibbutz

mother is somehow deprived. It all appears from the outside so regulated and structured, the bringing up of our children, I mean. It isn't like that at all. When my children were born, nobody came along and said, Hand them over to the children's house—or else. Do you know the advantage it is for a mother of a newborn babe to be able to put her baby to bed under the care of an expert nurse and get a few hours' sleep herself? Of course we can keep the baby at home if we wish. It's up to the mother. After giving birth, we have two months'

A kibbutz wedding is a community affair in which all join. The children's community enjoys first priority. It is equipped with every facility to enable the youngsters to pursue their own group development.

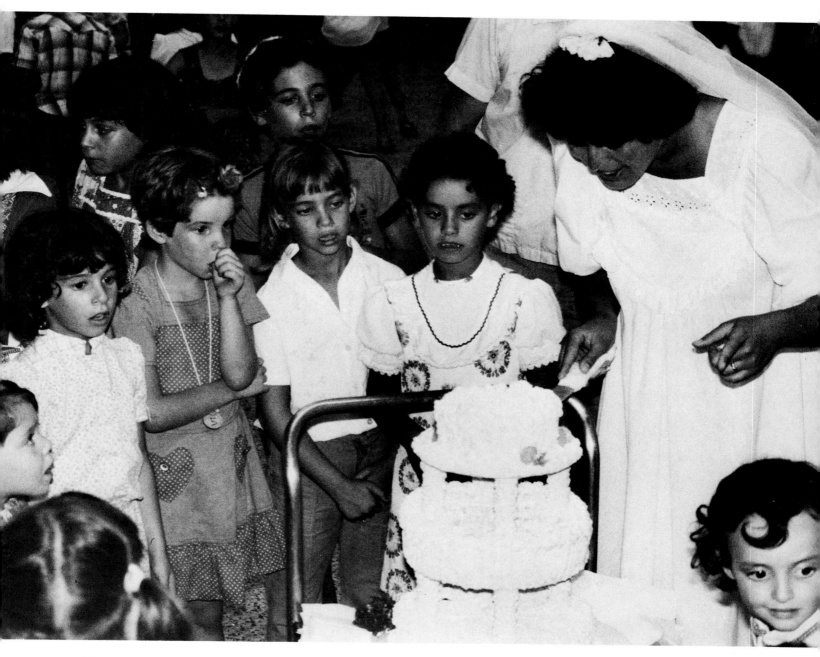

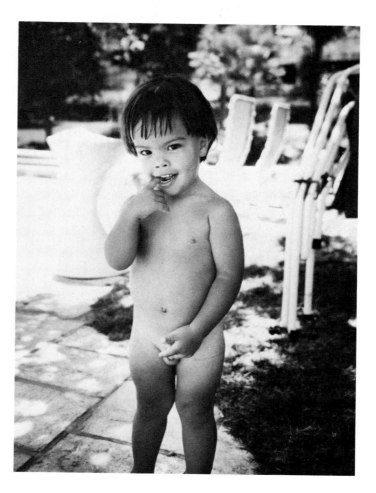

complete rest from work to devote to the baby and after that we only return to a full schedule gradually. How many women in town have that kind of an advantage? In the baby house the nurse is there to help and advise the mother—in feeding, bathing, that kind of thing. And even now, I can come and go to the nursery as I please. In the course of any normal working day I see the children on and off any number of times. I go to them, they pop in to see me. It's all so different from the textbook."

Not many miles away lives Tziviya. Her home is Tirat Zvi, once a mosquito-infested border settlement on the Jordan River and now a tree-shaded village set among its own orchards, fields, plantations, and fish-breeding ponds. It boasts one of the best meat-processing plants in the country. Tirat Zvi's summer climate is subtropical, too hot for the comfort of anyone not born there. Tziviya was, and this shows in her sun-drenched complexion and her easy native way of moving through the heat as she points out the features of her kibbutz school. Tziviya is just twenty, a third-generation kibbutznik and training to be a teacher. This and her kibbutz loyalties infuse her reflections with an almost aggressive conviction.

"I sometimes have the feeling that no group of youngsters anywhere has been so analyzed and dissected as us kibbutz kids. The literature by so-called experts from abroad can fill libraries and I think much of it is utter gibberish. I'm reading it in college. The things some of them write! Yes, I know, our mothers are supposed to be deprived and we are supposed to be emotionally shallow because we presumably grow up totally dependent on the children's community. I even read that we have no individual egos because they have all been drowned in the collective personality of the group. Bruno Bettleheim wrote something like that in that book on kibbutz youngsters so many people seem to have read—*Children of the Dream.* Look at me. Do I look like someone with a drowned ego? I have an opinion on everything!"

In Tziviya's view, it takes a kibbutznik to capture the subtleties of kibbutz life. The outsider, even the trained observer, can probe and analyze but can never enter the inner labyrinths of the child-parent relationships, which, according to her, are special.

"Believe me, they are different and better than in most families outside and there's good reason for it. When I was a youngster in the children's house and came home to my parents' room at the end of the working day—I was with them in every sense of the word. I wasn't just around them; I was really with them and they with me.

Remember, when a kibbutznik's day is done, it is really done. He doesn't have to worry about his next salary. That's what kibbutz is all about. Our fathers are more relaxed and our mothers are not harassed by the daily domestic routines of running a home. Our whole relationship—parents, brothers, sisters—is between people as people. Of course, there are exceptions but I think that we kibbutz families are closer than many I've seen on the outside.''

Tziviya's hard-hitting defense of the kibbutz family extends to the qualities of kibbutz youngsters. "To generalize and say, as those experts I've read have written, that we are shallow and ego-deprived is as stupid as saying that kibbutzniks are communists. Our kibbutz, Tirat Zvi, is religious, strictly Orthodox. One of the first permanent buildings we built was the synagogue. When I stand in front of a class of our kids, I can tell almost immediately by their behavior who their parents are. Their personalities are as different as children anywhere. And they are a far cry from being a docile, regimented lot. I don't say the kibbutz education is the best in the world, but it's almost. Where else," claims Tziviya, "does a child get such a commu-

From afar they all look of the same mold, but they are as individually different as children anywhere.

They grow up together almost
like brothers and sisters.

nity spirit and at the same time such a training in independent responsibilities from such an early age? And I'll say something else: I'll show you kids on the outside who hardly know their parents as anything but treadmill breadwinners, prisoners of the rat race. Well, if you want to get out of the rat race, join a kibbutz. Kibbutzniks generally die of old age, not of heart attacks."

The Israeli army authorities have done some studies of their own on kibbutz youngsters and they make interesting reading. It turns out that kibbutz teen-agers are particularly good officer material. They bring to the job, so the studies suggest, inbred characteristics that make for team spirit. The delegation of responsibility

comes naturally to them, they are used to field conditions, and have the stamina for hard work. They have a way with machines and are said to be capable of functioning independently with enterprise. They usually have a more than average educational background and are well-motivated. Thus, there is hardly another sector of the population which furnishes the Israel Defense Forces with such a high percentage of their officers. It is an almost natural dimension of kibbutz education with its emphasis on commitment and humanistic values. Read kibbutz journals and you discover columns written by their soldiering sons that sometimes sound like moralistic soul-searching confessionals.

Even after their army service is over, these young men and women are expected to give at least one additional year of voluntary service for the national good, whether as youth leaders in city youth movements or as reinforcements to help a new border kibbutz establish itself. After that they return home.

Not all do, however. Exposure to the world beyond the kibbutz inevitably seduces the fancy of some who go off to experiment with city life, to travel, or to embark on higher studies. The postarmy drop-out rate is a problem that can account in some kibbutzim for the departure of quite a high percentage of their youngsters, as many as fifty percent in some places. It is a problem that constantly engages parents, educators, and youngsters alike.

"Obviously," says Shimi, a final-year student at the Kibbutz Sde Eliyahu regional high school, "this question concerns some of us a lot. However much we, at our age, assure each other that in three

The kibbutz kindergartens and schools can afford small classes and much individual attention.

or four years' time, after our army and volunteer service is over, we shall all meet again back in kibbutz, we know that some of us will eventually leave. The statistics say so. The kibbutz has given us the best of everything. In ten years' time some of us will be running whole branches. I wouldn't want to live anywhere else or be something else. But how can I know for sure today whether I'll feel exactly this way in years to come?"

Shoshana echoes Shimi's self-questioning. She is in the same grade and it is clear from the way she speaks that she has thought hard about the matter. "Contrary to what people think," she explains, "there is a problem between the generations in the kibbutz. I don't want, for example, to come back after the army and find myself having to fight to go to university. There are still some old-timers who think it's a criminal thing to do, to go on to higher studies unless it's to learn a subject the kibbutz needs, like engineering or teaching or agriculture. I'm not sure what I would like to study but I don't want to be dictated to. I know that whether I stay or not will depend a great deal on that. It took years before our kibbutz high schools agreed to prepare us for university entrance exams and even today there are some who don't on principle. I honestly believe that in this day and age the kibbutz must allow anybody who wants to go on to university to do so. I remember the kind of friction there was in our kibbutz when I was a kid between the older and younger people over who would work where. Old-timers were reluctant to rotate their jobs—the skilled jobs—with the up-and-coming generation. It took time to work it out, until the adjustments were made and the problem was more or less settled. Well, I believe that just as that adjustment was made, the kibbutz—the whole kibbutz movement all over the country—will have to accommodate itself to the fact that very many kibbutz kids want to go on to university. The kibbutz still exists because it has always known how to adapt itself. This is going to be its next big adaptation."

Shoshana is probably right. The kibbutz high school postarmy generation is finding its way to universities in larger numbers than before. What this will do in terms of the community it is still too early to tell. But whatever form the evolution takes, it is certain that the kibbutz youth of the 1980s will carry into their society something of their own, just as every other kibbutz generation has done in the past. The future variations might not be as pastoral as the founders had envisaged but the kibbutz model will, assuredly, remain essentially unchanged.

Pear picking in the orchards of Lavi, a religious kibbutz in Lower Galilee.

VI

Sabra Tradition

Hillel, Aged Seventeen, Ramat Gan

I suppose one should know what the Jewish tradition is about because it's part of the heritage, but that doesn't mean one has to be religious. I'm not. I haven't really been inside a synagogue since my bar mitzvah except on Yom Kippur, and then not to pray; just to be there. Don't ask me why. I just feel it's the proper thing to do. My mother lights candles on Sabbath eve, but that's about all we do at home. I don't have any religious friends my age; we just don't mix. The only time I ever really spoke to religious kids was at a weekend seminar organized by Gesher (Bridge). That's the movement that brings religious and nonreligious high school kids together to discuss ideas. It was interesting. We need more of that kind of thing—to get together to discuss what it's all about and which way we sabras are going. Sometimes it gets a little confusing—the distinction between being an Israeli and a Jew and what ties we have to Jews outside Israel. Most of us don't think about it all that much, but when we do, the discussions are always heated. I envy religious kids in a way because they seem to have all the answers. I came away from that weekend seminar with the feeling that we nonreligious can afford to be what we are because the religious keep the tradition alive. I suppose that without that we wouldn't be Jews. Some at the seminar claimed that the religious were more patriotic than we are, that they were dedicated to Israel by religious commitment and were ready for greater self-sacrifices. I don't buy that. To me Israel is a normal country and you don't have to be observant to feel for your own country. Nevertheless, I must admit that those religious people who drop

181

everything to build settlements on the West Bank show tremendous idealism. I suppose the old pioneers must have been something like that in their day.

Sabras—how Jewish are they? Paradoxical as the question sounds, it has been a matter of public controversy, vocal and sometimes abrasive, for decades. There was even a time, in the 1950s, when anxiety ran rather deep that the Jewishness of many Jewish youngsters born in the Jewish state was actually developing outside the cultural identity of Judaism into a kind of national secular Hebrewism. Arthur Koestler, a renowned philosopher-writer of those years, provocatively predicted that it would take a generation or two, no more, before the Jewish people would undergo an irrevocable split: Israelis and Jews. Professor Ernst Simon, a highly respected Jerusalem scholar, caused a stir by his lengthy essay analyzing the contemporary spiritual scene and its very title—"Are We Israelis Still Jews?"—put the question unequivocally.

The 1950s were years when sabras—by no means the majority but also not just a peripheral few—would maintain that they were Israelis, not Jews, as though the one identity supplanted the other. It was not, for most, so much a matter of ideological doctrine, but rather a state of mind, a feeling, a mood, a self-image. With the battle for national independence over and done with, Israel was now a country

Facing the Western Wall, Jerusalem; a young nation steeped in ancient memories.

(*Opposite*) Carrying on the tradition: Many nonobservant parents want their children to have some appreciation of the religious heritage.

There was a time, in the early years of the state, when many sabras described themselves as Israeli, not Jewish. Those days are gone.

as normal as any other, these youngsters said. The anomaly of Jewish exile was at an end, and hence the religious heritage—which had kept the Jewish people alive even though homeless—was no longer indispensable. By all means, be Jewish if you wish, just as you may be an Israeli Christian or a Moslem or a member of any other faith for that matter. However, in the normalized nation-state called Israel what now counted was not religious identity but national identity, and being an Israeli was of itself identity enough. It required no elaboration, just as being an American or a British or an Italian or any nationality needed no addendum.

Some intellectuals went further by codifying the feeling into an ideology. They organized themselves into a movement which they called the "Canaanites," after the ancient name of the land before it became the Promised Land. Sabras, they said, were the successors of cultures born out of this soil since the dawn of history. The new Israeli state must seek its roots and pedigree in the civilizations originating in what began as Canaan and obliterate the "mongrel" identity exile had bred. They respected no particular parochial bond with, or responsibility toward, the culture or history or heritage of those who called themselves Jews. They, the "Canaanites," did not consider themselves Jews.

This attitude was not widespread, but its thrust—the feeling of detachment from the mainstream of Jewish life, peoplehood, tradition and history, and the affirmation of an exclusive Israeli ethnic personality—was shared to some degree by many young people. It was enhanced by the almost intoxicating novelty of national freedom and the anticipation of a new heritage in the making.

Such sabras, products of a secular and nationalistic education in the main, were actually acting out their own spontaneous, unrehearsed, and simplistic epilogue to the extraordinarily complex, enigmatic, long, and tragiheroic drama of the Jewish people. They were incapable of identifying emotionally with Jewry's centuries of exile for they had been taught to perceive it only as onerous and bad and humiliating, and they thus felt little or nothing in common with those who had not left it. They tried to write themselves out of its scenario by producing their own original Israeli script peopled by prototypes cast in their own national self-image. In their perception Israel's history was a two-tiered montage, the first ending with the freedom fighter, Bar Kockba, who led the final, futile revolt against Israel's Roman conquerors in A.D. 135, and the second beginning with the Bilu, the name of the first homeward-bound pioneer wave in 1882. Everything in between was a gray, nonsabra blank.

Zalman Aranne, Israel's minister of education and a respected reformer, pinpointed the dilemmas confronting Israel's secular educational philosophies. Addressing the Knesset in 1959, he said, "From the outset and throughout the decades the nation's schools have faced a variety of educational contradictions—how to educate Israeli youth with a deep attachment to the Jewish people when the largest part of that people lives outside Israel; how to inculcate into Israeli youth a sense of Jewish history when half of that history occurred outside the geography of Israel; how to convey to Israeli youth a feeling of Jewish consciousness when Israeli consciousness and the revolution it invoked have dictated not merely the rejection of the Jewish exile but also the rejection of Jewish Diaspora life; how to inculcate into Israeli youth in nonreligious schools the cultural heritage of the Jewish people when, throughout the generations, that heritage was immersed in religious faith."

Grappling with these predicaments and the ambivalent attitudes they produced aroused an ever-deepening sense of unease even within the secular establishment as more and more stories of sabra alienation came to the fore. One that made headlines was the Moscow youth festival of 1957. In the effort to woo and lull Western public opinion, the Russian propaganda machine occasionally engaged in displays of showmanship and one of them was an international festival for youth in Moscow. Israeli groups were invited to attend.

"Hear O Israel, the Lord Our God, the Lord is One." It was the ancient Jewish liturgy that did much to nurture the vision of a future national redemption out of which secular Zionism was born.

Authorities in Jerusalem seized upon the opportunity. Inside the Soviet Union were some three million Jews who, for decades, had been systematically choked by an official policy that deprived them of virtually every authentic mode of Jewish self-expression. They were allowed no freedom of contact or exchange with the Jewish world outside, and emigration to Israel or to anywhere else was barred. For hundreds of thousands of them the recently founded Jewish state was a distant beacon of light and hope. To be afforded an opportunity to see, just to see the offspring of that state on Russian soil would be a great comfort.

So, naturally, the few-score members of the Israeli delegation were carefully screened, spruced, and selected. The Jewish state, through its sabras, was going to send a message of love to the Russian Jewish community, telling them that they were not forgotten, that Israel was free and strove for their freedom, that all Jews were one and responsible for each other. The youngsters were being dispatched to Moscow to say shalom.

Clearly, the Soviet authorities would do their best to make sure the message was not delivered, by keeping the delegation away from the Jewish community. But there was one place and one time when official hindrance and harassment would, perforce, be more difficult to assert—the Moscow synagogue on Sabbath morning. Soviet secret police could hardly prevent the sabras from attending services. So, before leaving for Moscow, the youngsters were told to be sure to go to shul, to the synagogue, on the Sabbath morning of their stay. They went and Jews from all over Russia traveled from afar just to see them. On that Sabbath morning the usually sparse, aging Moscow congregation was augmented by an overflowing crowd, not of worshipers—for many had forgotten or had never been taught the language or order of service of Jewish prayer—but of spiritually starved spectators. Merely to stand and stare and drink in the sight of those bronzed, clear-eyed, fresh-looking, proud offspring of the sovereign Jewish state was enough.

But not for all.

It is a centuries-old custom of synagogal service for the congregation to call upon a guest to mount to the Torah reading-stand and recite the set blessing over the prescribed Torah text of the week. Every bar mitzvah boy knows that blessing by heart. It is a most solemn feature of the service.

Naturally, the Israeli youngsters were to be so honored but when their representatives were called to the reading stand, the Torah scroll open before them, they stood there, each in his turn, not sure what to do or say. They didn't know the Torah blessing. These sabras had never been inside a synagogue in their lives before. They simply did not know custom or ritual or tradition—those cherished practices of the Jewish heritage sanctified by time and handed down from generation to generation within portals which, throughout the centuries, had perpetuated Jewish identity, existence, and spiritual survival—the synagogue.

(*Opposite*) A collective bar-mitzvah ceremony for orphans of the wars.

188

Veteran congregants watched in shocked silence. That their own youth should be estranged from the heritage and traditions was axiomatic and sad. But that the children of Israel, of the Jewish state, should not know—that was inexplicable. Whereby were they Jewish? some people asked.

"We were bewildered," recalls Grischa Moscowitz, now of Na-

thanya but then a young Leningrad Jew from one of the relatively few families still observant. "I had traveled specially with a friend to see them. We so much wanted to set our eyes on those sabras, just to get a picture of what they looked like. To us they appeared splendid. But then, when that happened with the Torah reading, I felt terribly let down, as if the secret police had played a dirty trick on us. I remember thinking to myself, if the Jewish state has given up being Jewish, what's the point of remaining Jewish in Russia?"

When the news of that Sabbath morning service reached Israel,

(Preceding pages) The Western Wall is the last remnant of the temple the Romans destroyed. Each year, on the anniversary of the catastrophe, people of every degree of observance assemble to recite lamentations over the disaster that precipitated the national exile. Some sit on the ground as a sign of mourning.

(Right) The Wall is both a synagogue and a national shrine. In the words of one sage: "There are stones that are hearts and hearts that are stones."

it created something of a furor. It exposed a painful controversy, long in the making, over the educational philosophies of the nation. Israel had always been ideologically polarized between religious and nonreligious with a strong antireligious representation on the far left. Parents had the choice of sending their children either to religious schools where they received a manifestly Orthodox education or to nonreligious schools where they received no traditional education at all. Approximately two thirds of the youth attended the general, nonreligious school system, and the sabra delegation to Moscow was mainly its products. Post-Independence Israel was reaping the educational harvest sown by its secular founding fathers at the turn of the century. Their doctrines had been revolutionary enough to forge statehood but they evidently were not traditional enough to preserve the peoplehood.

Religious thinkers were among the ranks of the early Zionist patriarchs, but the most dominant and influential voices came from the secular ideologues. The secularists of the turn of the century embodied a modern prophecy of a new Judaism.

Historically and traditionally, Judaism had always meant faith and peoplehood, the one deriving from the other and the two inextricably bound together—what scholars have called a nation-religion. It stood to reason that were it not for the fierce attachment of the Jewish people to their faith, there could be no perpetuation of the Jewish nation. Judaism was always a composite of God and people bound by a covenant and enacted through a behavioral discipline prescribed by religious law. Expelled from the country of their origin, the Jews had stayed alive as one nation in history despite their nineteen centuries of dispersion by loyalty to that discipline. Throughout, the thrust of Judaism's studies, laws, symbols and traditions, its festivals and days of mourning, its prayers and scholarly texts, were profoundly dramatic reminders to the people of their roots in the Land of Israel and of the messianic hope of an ultimate return to it.

However, this spiritual bond of attachment began to be assailed as secularism made ever stronger inroads into European Jewish society, beginning in the eighteenth and intensifying in the nineteenth century. No Western nation was immune to its influence, but in the case of the Jews the consequences were especially complex since history only knew Judaism—and the Jews only knew themselves—as a nation-religion. The notion of a person defining himself at one and the same time as Jewish and secular was unheard of. To give up the practice of the faith meant, ipso facto, surrendering up the passport to the people. Indeed, many Jews did surrender when ultimately faced with the quandaries of choice presented by the political and civic freedoms and equalities which emancipation in nineteenth-century Europe offered them. They assimilated. Others reformed Judaism into a theological persuasion unrelated to peoplehood just as Christianity contains no element of peoplehood. However, the masses, including most of the irreligious, rejected these courses. They refused to surrender the ethnic legitimacy of their blood tie, and the intellectuals among them launched a popular movement of Jewish "enlightenment" which strove to cast the ancient civilization into a modern cultural mold. It was in this climate that the Zionist secular idea took root.

Among its most persuasive proponents were mainly Russian Jews who, though they had abandoned the tradition and were influenced in many cases by the new trends of socialism, rejected assimilation as a solution to the Jewish dilemmas of the day. Their formula was nationalism. They preached the doctrine of a Jewish national destiny without God. They advocated peoplehood and sovereignty without theology. They wrote a literature that reinterpreted historic Judaism, separating nationality from religion; the latter was a matter of faith, the former a matter of fact. This was their intellectual revolution—the detheologization of Judaism and, in its place, the perpetuation of the heritage and the people through the reconstitution of the Jewish nation-state. What religion had done to maintain the self-identity of the people in exile would now be guaranteed by the territorial concentration in the Land of Israel, by the rootedness in its soil, by the revival of the Hebrew language and the nurturing of a Hebrew culture, by the community of purpose; in short, by all those attributes of nationhood that normal sovereignty offers—land, language, community, and culture. National survival and Jewish eternity were no longer functions of faith.

But what of the ancient religious tradition whose sons these innovators were, so many of them the rebellious products of the eastern European yeshiva world? They had to cling to that tradition, for it was their identity; they were children of its spirit and value-system and they understood that without it there could be no Zionism, no Jewish eternity, no Jews. So, by the logic of their creed, they set about secularizing it, investing it with a purely cultural and folk content responsive and relevant to the revived nationalist spirit and the return to the homeland and its soil. Scholarly volumes philosophizing, conceptualizing, and reinterpreting the old religious texts, customs, and festivals were written. The early pioneer settlements became the principal crucible of the new cultural alchemy. What had been a messianic yearning for redemption now became an inner will for national self-determination. What had been the holy Sabbath was now a socialist social institution determining the working man's inherent right to a day's rest. The Haggadah, the sanctified Passover eve narrative telling of the Exodus from Egypt, was rewritten as a story of the birth and renewal of a nation, not as God's intervention in history. Yom Kippur became a day of community introspection, not of fasting and prayer. The feasts of Tabernacles, Passover, and Pentecost became folk harvest festivals. The Bible remained supreme; but it remained supreme as the national treasure and not as the word of God by God. It was now the source book of the nation's cultural heritage, history, language, literature, and humanistic values, and the title deed of the Jewish people to the ancient Jewish homeland.

One who remembers those days of almost frenzied ideological experiment, when God and pioneer were a contradiction in terms, is octogenarian Miriam Zinger. Israel knows her as an author of children's books who came to Degania in 1920 as a kindergarten teacher. Then, eight children played in a thatched structure under the old cherub tree. This was her kindergarten and this is what she told an interviewer on the occasion of Degania's seventieth anniversary in 1980:

"I remember that the 'Russian' influence dominated everything. It was forbidden to mention the name of God. One day a kibbutz member was injured and the children asked me where do people come from that they are so easily broken? One youngster jumped up and said, 'From monkeys.' Another, a little girl, said, 'From God.' I then sat the children down and conducted a miniature poll. Most votes went to God, but one child, a little girl, said, 'I, too, think that people come from monkeys but that monkeys were created by God.' From then on I began to tell them Bible stories and afterwards the kibbutz asked me to conduct a pedagogic seminar for the valley settlements round about. I agreed on one condition—that I be allowed to open the seminar with a talk on 'Children and God.' They accepted and in that talk I explained how the child conceives God in nature. Subsequently, one left-wing newspaper wrote an article condemning me as 'that religious kindergarten teacher.' "

Such were the prevalent moods of the day. Religion was a thing of the past, a ghetto burden good for the ghetto Jew. The sabras—the new liberated Jews—needed none of that. The revived Hebrew language they spoke and read, the people who jostled them day by day, the biblical landscape that surrounded them on every side, the national struggle—everything, everywhere told them who they were, whence they came, and where they were going. They did not need the synagogue once a week or once a year, nor did they need the anti-Semite to remind them of their identity. Merely by being the children of the nation's cultural and political renaissance they were rejuvenated Jews.

How wrong they were, those brave, ingenious, optimistic, idealistic pioneer Zionist secularists. Hardly was their national battle done and the 1948 War of Independence won when it appeared that something had gone wrong. Some sabras were growing up into a breed never intended. Secular Zionism had never thought to supplant the old, deep Jewish root by a shallow Israeli newcomer. What they had set out to do was to take the original out of what they considered to be the claustrophobic, tormented hothouse of the exile and transplant it back into its natural soil and setting, there to be refreshed and reinvigorated by the energy and light of national freedom. No-

A thirteen-year-old receiving the Torah and, with it, the responsibilities of his heritage.

body had wanted to secularize Judaism to death, which, by the 1950s, is what seemed to be starting to happen.

To many educators, parents, and public representatives, themselves reared on the classic secular, humanist, Zionist, nationalist doctrines, the 1957 incident in the Moscow synagogue became a watershed in the grand national debate that had been going on for years, prodded and fueled constantly by the religious establishment. What this and so many other similar episodes of sabra ignorance of and alienation from Judaism did was to awaken mainstream Israel to the truth that no nation can censor its history or edit its heritage; that no nation can be robbed of its ancestral mystique—that inner soul of uninterrupted tradition which, link by link, binds present to past and endows a people with self-perpetuation, self-conception, self-identity, self-confidence, self-respect. In the case of the Jewish nation, self-respect and identity commanded an understanding, if not an observance, of the sanctified traditions of the ancient faith which was and remains the bedrock of universal Jewish oneness.

Thus it was that by the late 1950s a new curriculum was devised for the nonreligious schools—the "Jewish consciousness" program. Its major architect was Minister of Education Aranne and its declared aim was not religious indoctrination, but "to develop a sympathetic understanding for the traditional forms of Jewish life." Youngsters were at last shown what a synagogue looks like, what a Torah scroll is, and the procedures of service. They were introduced to religious customs, commandments, and thought, to the sacred meaning of the festivals and to the content of the prayer books. They began to learn of the cultural treasures written during the exile, of the great philosophers, scholars, and poets the exile had produced. In short, they were now being shown their own roots.

Over the years the program has been developed and amended many times and, of course, it has its critics both from the left and the right. To this day parents who want to ensure that their children receive a thoroughly religious education still send them to religious schools. But the very integration of the "Jewish consciousness" program into the general secular school system articulates the agreement of the nation's overwhelming majority that they want their children to have an appreciation of Judaism and its heritage, even if they are not observant, and that they absolutely disown any identity that would separate their children from the universal Jewish one. They want Israel to be a Jewish state, not merely a state of Jews.

How Jewish?—this remains the overriding question of Israeli society. It is rare today to come across teen-agers who will declare themselves to be Israelis not Jews, and the "Canaanite" cult, too, has withered with the times. That schizophrenic interlude, which was a little frightening, is all but over. Not so, however, is the controversy over the extent to which traditional religious norms should be legislated into national life. This argument goes on unabated and often heatedly. Conceivably, it will never stop, for Israel is a democracy not a theocracy and its Jews represent every hue from the religious far right to the political far left.

Some complain of too much religion in the public domain and others fret that there is far too little. There are groups who demand more prerogatives for the rabbinic authorities and groups who decry those they already have. But raucous though these extremes are, they tend to be mellowed within the majority mainstream, that multiple admixture which stands somewhere between the sworn theocrats and the sworn atheists and is often at loggerheads with both. The people of the center make no pretensions to consistency and most of Israel's youngsters are their heirs.

These are the children from families who enjoy the beaches on a Sabbath morn and who solemnly light candles on a Sabbath eve; who rarely attend synagogue but seek religious instruction for bar mitzvah; who concur with the Sabbath ban on public transport but drive their own vehicles without compunction; who buy kosher meat from the local butcher but do not necessarily maintain kosher homes; who insist that circumcision, marriage, divorce, and burial are the rightful province of the rabbis but are unsympathetic toward rabbinic meddling in politics; who enjoy Friday night television yet do not really object to the closure of public places of entertainment on Sabbaths and festivals; who want the schools to teach the children tradition but not so much as to make a nuisance of themselves at home. This is an undefined, disparate consensus group ranging from traditionalists with no penchant for dogmatics, to practitioners who are unabashed compromisers, to fellow travelers who are patently inconsistent, to secularists with a religious nostalgia, and to nonbelievers sensitive to the susceptibilities of believers. These are the people who do not want to be arbitrarily fettered by religious injunctions in their private lives but who are not averse to the infusion of tradition in public life. They want Israel to look Jewish.

Doron comes from such a home. He is a ginger-haired lad from Rehovot, south of Tel Aviv, and he is in his final high school year. His school is nonreligious. Lean and tall, his deep-set blue eyes are encased in a sharply chiseled face peppered with freckles. His whole countenance reflects intelligence. He says:

"One problem is that all of us in Israel wear badges. If you wear a *kippa* [a skullcap] you are marked religious and if you don't you're ostensibly an agnostic or an atheist. That's nonsense. Gone are the days when you could divide people into observant and antiobservant, religious and antireligious. I hardly keep anything but I don't feel irreligious. When I'm in Jerusalem, I enjoy going to the Western Wall. Its authenticity says something to me. I pray in my own way, not from a prayer book, but it's genuine prayer nevertheless. And I don't think I'm exceptional. We don't want Israel to be a clerical state but we don't want to be dictated to by the rabid secularists, either. If you were to take a poll among my friends, I think most would say they have a respect for tradition and that tradition has to be a part of our national life. I'm talking about keeping some semblance of a public Sabbath and festivals, keeping the army kosher, observing Yom Kippur, things like that."

Esther is a school friend of Doron in the same grade. She is precocious-looking, small, brunette, and very attractive. She speaks

with a husky voice that every now and again reveals a slight mid-
western American accent when she pronounces certain vowels. Her
parents came from Cleveland, Ohio, when she was fourteen. This is
her perspective:

"There's just no comparison between here and over there in
America, none at all. In America, if one wants to stay Jewish one has
to work at it, I mean really work at it. Our home wasn't particularly
religious and I went to public school, not a parochial one. My only
Jewish education was the Sunday school once a week and occasional
Friday night services. Frankly, I hardly learned a thing; how much
can one possibly learn a few hours a week? I knew no Hebrew beyond a few prayers and got a little bit of Bible and Jewish history and
that's about all. By the time I was thirteen, I left Sunday school along
with most of my friends. That was the extent of my Jewish education
and I don't think I was atypical. Kindergarten kids in Israel have a
greater knowledge of Jewish culture than most adult Jews in America.
That's what I mean when I say that over there, if you want to remain

Jewish and you don't want your kids to intermarry and assimilate, you have to consciously work at it day and night—education, home, environment, temple, everything. You have to actually be at it all the time to remain different, to remain Jewish. Here I don't have to be different at all. I just have to be me and that's why my parents came to live here. Being Jewish in Israel is natural. We take it for granted, without hang-ups, because the whole environment is Jewish. We learn Bible in school as a normal part of the curriculum, along with geography and Jewish consciousness and Jewish history and math. The whole street is Jewish—not all religious, but Jewish.''

Be in Israel on a Yom Kippur and you see Esther's contention manifested in an extreme degree. No law prohibits private motorists on the roads, yet the highways and the streets are silent, empty of traffic. Everything, even the radio and television, shuts down. It

There are some old-world Eastern European-style neighborhoods, intensely Orthodox, living their own lives apart. One such community is Mea Shearim (the Hundred Gates), Jerusalem.

would seem that most people fast and those who do not don't advertise it. The synagogues are packed, filled with people who come to pray or who come to share in the solemnity of the hour or who simply come because Jews have always assembled together on Yom Kippur.

Be in Israel during the Passover week and you find a virtually breadless country. Bakers take their leave as the nation consumes matzoh, the unleavened wafers which the children of Israel ate when they left Egypt. The Passover eve ritual is universally respected as the great annual family get-together, its focus on the children as tradition dictates. It is the hour for the generations to come together around a single table and recite the Haggadah, the traditional Exodus story. Even in nonreligious kibbutzim the hallowed text is no longer rewritten and secularized. The old narrative is back—sometimes

Purim is carnival time, celebrating salvation from Haman, a Hitler-like Persian tyrant of centuries ago. It is a festival replete with drama, romance, and intrigue; and like most of the traditional festivals it has both a religious and a national character.

brought up to date to include contemporary chapters—and the old songs are sung deep into the night.

Be in Israel on Sukkoth, the Feast of Tabernacles, when balconies, patios, and courtyards exhibit those fragile booths, loosely thatched and colorfully decorated, built to last a week in commemoration of the temporary habitations of the children of Israel during their forty years' sojourn in the desert. Many a nonobservant home builds a sukkah, a booth, for the pleasure of their children.

Be in Israel on a regular Sabbath and you sense the peace of the day. Factories, offices, shops, and places of entertainment shut down and the roads are relatively empty—until that hour when the nonobservant set out on their excursions. Israelis work a six-day week and the Sabbath is their single day of leisure.

Switch on the radio as every new day begins and you hear a brief morning prayer. Tune in at the evening peak hour and you hear the recitation of a Bible chapter and a scholar's interpretation of its meaning. Watch television at the day's end and an announcer shares with you a Torah text or a sage's thought. Read the press on each festival eve and you find columns of commentary relating the significance of the day to the reality of the hour. Be in Israel on Independence Day and you may watch live on television one of the country's most popular annual events—the international Bible quiz for youth.

This and more is the public tapestry of tradition in which Israel's youngsters grow up. The scene is composed of ancient wisdoms and practices which only the most religious strictly observe but which indelibly tint the spiritual strands of society. It is from such traditions that Israel's broad Jewish heritage provides the people with identity and distinction. Its expression is by no means uniform but the thread is enduring and it appears to be becoming imperceptibly stronger year by year. The Jewish state is probably not more religiously observant than it was two, three, and four decades ago, but it is manifestly more Jewish.

During the restless decades that preceded and consummated the Independence, to have been an average religious youngster was not only to be in a minority but also to be made to feel it. These children had a problem. The girls and boys who went to the religious nationalist youth movements and schools were enthusiastic patriots, no different from the rest, but they were in search of heroes, of Galahads they could call their own. All the great names of the national struggle had risen from the secular Zionist ranks. The Ben-Gurions, the Golda Meirs, the Dayans—these were the charismatic personalities who embodied the pioneer heroism and national fortitude, who spoke in the name of the people to the world, who personified the high drama, and who captured the imagination of the young. Yet none of them went to synagogue or put on phylacteries in the morning or observed the Sabbath day to keep it holy. None personally exemplified the model religious youngsters were taught from birth to emulate as the only legitimate, authentic, and superior Jewish way of life. So, orphaned of acknowledged national giants of their own, religious teen-agers adopted and identified with those admired by everybody else and this gave them something of an inferiority complex.

Take, for instance, the telling matter of the *kippa,* the yarmulke or skullcap, traditionally worn by strictly observant males, young and old. In the decades before Independence, religious boys did not parade them in public. It was just not done. The accepted headwear outdoors was a dark blue beret or a gray peaked cap. To be seen on the streets with a *kippa* on the head was to be conspicuous and, given the prevailing secular ideologies of the day, it was considered in some places ridiculous.

Take, also, the telling matter of the religious high schools. The capacity of many of them to reinforce the education of the home and keep teen-age youth observant was abysmal. Religious youngsters wanted pride, recognition; they wanted to belong and not to be different. Frustrated, many took off their berets and peaked caps and joined the widely hailed secular youth elite outside.

The founding years of the religious-kibbutz movement is another example. Its young men and women were relative latecomers to the pioneer scene (their first settlement was established only in 1936), but once they began, they seemed to move with a vengeance. They volunteered to build their settlements in the most hazardous, isolated, and out-of-the-way locations as though purposefully trying to drive home the point that they were making up for lost time, that they were as good as, if not better than, the rest. They were to pay a high price for their valor, for when war came, their outposts were on the first line of the onslaught and their casualties were heavy. At one of their kibbutz villages in the Hebron hills—Kfar Etzion—all but three of their menfolk were massacred.

It was sometime in the early 1960s that the *kippa* began to appear openly on the streets, worn mainly by the boys of the largest religious Zionist youth movement. Their skullcap design—finely knitted with a patterned edge—was distinctive and conspicuous.

They wore them white on Sabbath, to match their shirts. Within a very short while the style caught on across the country and the berets and peaked caps were thrown away. Here, if anything, was a signal that a new mood was afoot, that something important was evolving within the ranks of religious youth, potent enough to influence their self-image. It was not by chance that their apparent display of public self-confidence, symbolized by the *kippa,* coincided with the progressive introduction of the "Jewish consciousness" curriculum into the nonreligious schools. For, as the once widely accepted certainties of the old secularist isms began to be questioned and found somewhat wanting, the religious youngsters became ever less apologetic. They were now beginning to assert their own public identity, show their own flag—the *kippa*—and they did so with an increasing pride and even ostentation. They were becoming emancipated. The day of the "knitted *kippa* generation," as these youngsters are still called, had arrived.

The growth of the yeshiva-high school system and of the religious youth movements from whose ranks the system emerged had a lot to do with the changing face of mainstream religious youth. By the mid-fifties not a few of the run-of-the-mill religious secondary schools were in the doldrums, fighting a losing battle against the popular secular trends. It was then that some young rabbis, strongly Zionist, and youth leaders and parents, pressed ahead with a totally new concept that was ultimately to revolutionize much of the religious secondary education in the country—the yeshiva-high school. Nothing less than bastions of intense religious indoctrination could equip modern religious sabras for religious Zionist life—that life which was an amalgam of pioneering and piety and which toiled to integrate religious norms into the body politic of the Jewish state.

Mainly residential, they combined intensive yeshiva (Talmudic) studies with a secular high school education. Soon they began to attract the cream of religious youth and by the mid-sixties they and their variants (including parallel institutions for girls) became the backbone of the religious secondary school enterprise in the country. Many a graduate was to emerge more religiously scholastic and piously observant than his or her parents.

Israel's army is a highly flexible structure with a genius for adjusting its military needs to educational goals that serve the national interest. Thus, just as it accommodated itself to the kibbutz-oriented youth movements by creating Nahal, a pioneer military framework in which recruits could volunteer to build, till, and guard strategic border agricultural outposts, so it created a special army-cum-yeshiva framework for yeshiva-high school graduates. It came to be known as Hesder (Arrangement). By signing on for four or five years instead of the usual three, these graduates could perform their military training and battle duties interspersed with set periods of study in recognized Hesder yeshivoth. And again, it was the cream of the religious youngsters, highly motivated and idealistic, who chose this Arrangement as their army service.

It was the aftermath of the Six Day War that catapulted the "knitted *kippa* generation" into national recognition. In the eyes of many they were looked upon as the new elite.

"Suddenly we became a kind of an aristocracy with heroes all of our own," recalls Shmuel Hankin of Jerusalem, a teacher who was a yeshiva-high school pupil in 1967. "What the school gave us was deep conviction and religious pride. What the Six Day War gave us was the whole of biblical Eretz Israel, from the Jordan River to the Mediterranean Sea, and that to us was a miracle. We were resolved to settle the land, to go out and build new villages, to give up everything for the sake of what to us was a sacred task—the settlement of the liberated parts of Eretz Israel. To us it was a mitzvah, a religious commandment. By carrying this out, we saw ourselves as part of the grand messianic scheme. This was the logical climax of all the education we had received and important people began to applaud us."

Indeed, they won admiration and their settlement zeal gained the support of some of the nation's most prominent personalities—Begin, Dayan, Ezer Weizman, Ariel Sharon—the leadership which advocated that whatever the final political solution to the Arab-Israeli conflict, the Land of Israel must remain whole and not be divided again. This sabra youth established what soon became the highly controversial Gush Emunim (the Block of the Faithful), the movement of religious activists bent on the settlement of the mountains of Judea and Samaria, the West Bank.

By no means are all religious sabras fellow travelers of Gush Emunim, yet its philosophies are undeniably dominant. As for the nonreligious public—the majority—some support and most oppose its practices and creed. And yet many people will acknowledge, however grudgingly, that its spirit of fierce patriotism and idealism is the stuff that once built the nation. They would like to see something of it rub off on all the youth but without the mystic extravagance.

Girls from modern religious homes, schools, and youth movements interact with the boys in pursuing the tasks which their shared educational philosophies emphasize. They are not passive and are often pacesetters. The meeting ground of the girls with the boys is usually the youth movement, not the schools (for these are mostly segregated), and here in the clubhouse they socialize freely. (It is these religious girls who knit the skullcaps for the boys, often with the intention of delivering a personal message.)

The fashions of feminine modesty have grown somewhat stricter over the years, probably a reflection of the deepened religious convictions. Like very many sabras, these religious young ladies enjoy folk dancing, but at the youth movement clubhouse it is the convention for the dancing circles to remain separate, girls and boys apart. This, however, appears in no way to inhibit their boisterous styles and rhythms, for they carry into their steps something of the

Children of the ultra-Ortho-
dox: Their language is Yiddish and their secular studies
are limited to the three R's.

classic Hassidic fervor—that lively joy—imbibed from their religious upbringing.

Girls from such families usually wear skirts rather than slacks (except perhaps in the privacy of the home) and the more orthodox the upbringing the longer the dress and sleeve. All religious girls are granted exemption from army duties on religious grounds, a privilege that is not viewed sympathetically by the nonreligious society. However, many an eighteen-year old from middle-of-the-road religious families will choose army service on principle, joining a religious Nahal pioneer settlement unit, or serving as a teacher in uniform or entering any branch the military authorities see fit. The majority perform their national service in a civilian capacity—in hospitals, development towns, and slum areas. The extreme orthodox opt out completely from national service and they invariably marry very young.

As for the varied personal life-styles of the religious boys, the *kippa* says it all. For the kippa, in its multiple shapes, fabrics, and colors, is a sophisticated sign-language which, if read properly, spells out the way of life of its wearer. There are among Israeli youth as many skullcap styles as there are religious behavior patterns. Stand by a downtown bus-stop as the queues gather and the chances are you will see a *kippa* parade whose innuendos it takes years of practice to fathom.

Thus, the lad with the knitted *kippa* so small and of a color that so matches the hair as to make the skullcap almost invisible will presumably doff it entirely once he is rid of his religious high school discipline. The lad wearing the colored middle-size one with the patterned fringe (invariably pinned to the hair at a cocky angle) is, in all likelihood, a yeshiva-secondary school student (or one of its high school variants) and belongs to a religious youth movement. The lad standing with the small colored cloth one perched haphazardly on the top of his head can be taken as a regular religious high school student who prefers a clubhouse to a religious pioneer youth movement. The fellow with the very large knitted one bordered by a vivid pattern is almost certainly a Gush Emunim enthusiast. The fellow with the plain, very coarsely knitted one that virtually covers his whole skull is, one can bet, a repentant newcomer to deep religious observance. (If his hair is longer than normal, then you can take it that, as likely as not, he is from an American assimilated home.) The

tells much about the family's way of life.

lad with the black cloth one together with the fellow wearing its velvet equivalent are from particularly orthodox backgrounds and will go on to spend a few years at an advanced yeshiva of higher learning. One of them may even enter the rabbinate. And then there is the boy in the large white crocheted one with the little bob on top. It almost totally conceals the top of his head, shaved except for the flowing side curls around the ears. This is the youngster of the most orthodox community of all, from the Hassidic sects mainly, who live their own lives in their own way in their own neighborhood, separated from the world outside.

One such neighborhood is the Mea Shearim (the Hundred

Gates) quarter in Jerusalem, or the town of Bnei Brak near Tel Aviv, or a score of any other of these intensely orthodox old-world enclaves whose atmosphere is of utter piety, unadulterated by the caprices of modern life. This is a world of old-style yeshivas and very large families, of schools where the children are tutored in Yiddish and where, but for the three Rs, the whole curriculum is Talmud and Bible and religious commandments. It is a world of beards and side curls, of black hats and long coats, where women cover their heads and where little girls wear thick stockings. On Sabbath the streets are blocked off to all traffic, the silence punctuated only by the sound of prayer and traditional mealtime songs and the lilting chant of Talmudic

The traditional burning of the last of the bread on Passover Eve.

Scenes in a Hassidic enclave—compact societies where the lilting chant of Talmudic study fills the air, where beards and side curls are the norm and where the stranger is told not to enter immodestly dressed.

study. The men have a medieval eastern European look in their traditional fur-trimmed hats, and the women in their long dresses resemble sepia photographs from a grandmother's picture album. These are the neighborhoods where posters cover the walls beseeching visiting ladies to dress modestly and exhorting the local residents to protest some latest alleged outrage of the "Zionist state." For it is in these relatively small but compact quarters of extreme orthodoxy that you find some who, on grounds of deeply held theological conviction, protest the very existence of Israel. Israel, to them, is a man-made entity, and by definition it is an abomination that stands in the path of the messianic redemption to come, to be wrought by God alone.

Listen to Moishe, aged ten, from Jerusalem's Mea Shearim quarter. His side curls are blond, his big round eyes light blue. His trousers, held up by suspenders, reach down to below the knees and his long brown socks end in dusty boots. He wears a black broad-brimmed hat and his white crocheted skullcap sticks out at the back. His long-sleeved gray flannel shirt is buttoned to the neck and he carries a large Talmud tome whose edges are frayed from years of use. What he says echoes a way of life that some would call a static replica of the shtetl, of the eastern European Jewish hamlet of a century ago. But to Moishe, Mea Shearim is home. It is a place of living warmth and of the security of God's truth.

Moishe speaks in Yiddish. "I've only traveled once outside Jerusalem. I was very little then. I remember lots of big bonfires and torches and lots of men singing and dancing all night in the open. There were thousands and thousands of them and I clapped and sang on my father's shoulders. All day long we had driven in a special bus to a place called Meron in the mountains. Buses from everywhere came filled with fathers and boys my age. Everybody came to have their hair cut. Simeon ben Yohai is buried in Meron—he was a big important rabbi in the Talmud. After it got dark and the fires were lit, my father, like everybody else, took a big pair of scissors and he cut off all my hair, every bit of it except for the side curls. That is the custom, to have your hair cut off for the first time at Meron. All the fathers cut off all the curls of all the sons except for the side curls. The Torah says to do it. The Torah says you must never cut the sides and when you grow up you must grow a beard. And in three years' time when I'm bar mitzvah, I'll go to the yeshiva. I'll go to the yeshiva my father went to and where my grandfather went and where my brothers go. I'll learn there all the time—in Yiddish. In Mea Shearim we only speak Yiddish because Hebrew is holy and only the Zionists speak Hebrew. We don't have much to do with those people because they're not religious. Even the religious ones are not really religious like us. They don't grow beards like they should and they read gentile books and they go into the army. It's against the Torah to stop learning and go into the army. My teacher said so. He says Israel is against the Torah because only the Messiah can rebuild Jerusalem and the Temple. And when that happens, all the Jews from all over the world will come back to Eretz Israel and everybody will be religious like us."

Israel's children are presumably destined always to grow up in

From father to son—an unbroken chain of strict tradition.

a country seized by the enigmas and peculiarities of its unique historic origins—suspended between its ancient yesterday and its modern tomorrow, between tradition and innovation, between religious passion and secular rationalism, between Jewish statehood and Jewish diaspora, between a faith that is a people and a people that is not all faith. This is what makes the nation's contemporary spiritual panorama so full of intense contradictions and immense inner complexities. It is a patchwork of harmonies and conflicts, of similarities and polarities that must perforce occur within a restored nationhood that is but thirty-odd years old, born of a people whose tradition has lasted four thousand years.

Afterword

To its children the Jewish state is not a national novelty; it is the natural condition of their lives. They live by a routine that is as normal as that of youngsters in most other places—schools to attend, examinations to pass, romances to pursue, chores to do, games to play, parental disciplines to obey, and all the other elements in the kaleidoscope of experience that goes by the name of growing up. They are by nature as carefree as children can possibly be and sometimes more so, given those sabra traits that are often charmingly refreshing and occasionally exasperating, such as their earthy frankness (which can sound like rudeness) and their excessive exuberance (which can, at times, look like bad manners).

By any standard, sabras are an uninhibited crowd, not quite the breed, perhaps, the founding fathers had envisaged, although a good many of them come fairly close to the image. But then, the founders' dream did not harbor nightmares. Sweat, toil, and some tears, yes, but not the torment that devastated such a large number of the Jewish people on the eve of statehood, nor the trials which accompanied the birth of the Jewish state and the wars and tensions which followed after that. On the way to freedom, disastrously violent eruptions occurred whose tremors have never really ceased, and these were not accounted for—not to such a degree—in the original classic Zionist doctrines. Nor were the international anomalies—and sometimes solitude—which have shaped Israel's fortunes within the family of nations. The children of the Jewish state, therefore, may well model the liberation of spirit generated from within, but they are not totally immune to the problems imposed by vicissitudes from without—and some of these are classically Jewish.

The literature of the early Zionist thinkers and philosophers of the turn of the century, those who formulated the doctrines and shaped the concepts of the return of the Jews to Zion, presents a single major hypothesis: A Jewish state is a necessity because the Jewish historical condition without it is an aberration, an abnormality. History had turned Jews into a freak nation. Here was a people, they argued, an authentic and an ancient people, exiled from their land, scattered and homeless, despised and vilified, and all because they did not have a country of their own. Every Jewish affliction, every irrational accusation ever directed against the Jews—causing the Black Plague, the Great Fire of London, the Russian crop failure; poisoning wells; drinking the blood of gentile children—every mad prejudice stemmed from this source, homelessness. Leo Pinsker, an outstanding Zionist philosopher, put it this way in his classic treatise, *Auto-emancipation,* written in 1882:

Among the living nations of the earth the Jews occupy a position of a nation long since dead. With the loss of the homeland, the Jews lost their independence and fell into a state of decay which is incompatible with the existence of a whole and vital organism. The state was crushed by Roman conquerors and vanished from the world's view. But after the Jewish people had yielded up its existence as an actual state, as a political entity, it could nevertheless not submit to total destruction—it did not cease to exist as a spiritual nation. Thus, the world saw in this people the frightening form of one of the dead walking among the living. This ghostlike apparition . . . this eerie form scarcely paralleled in history, unlike anything that preceded it or followed it, could not fail to make a strange and peculiar impression upon the imagination of the nations. And if the fear of ghosts is something inborn, and has a certain justification in the psychic life of humanity, is it any wonder that it asserted itself powerfully at the sight of this dead and yet living nation?

Not everybody agreed with this diagnosis, but virtually all the Jewish nationalist thinkers of the day arrived at the same conclusion, that the Jewish people must normalize itself, must rehabilitate itself, by creating for itself what every other normal nation possesses—a country. Given that, and its regenerating political, cultural, social, and economic identities—a flag, an army, a government, a cohesive nationhood with its own language and culture, working its own soil

225

They chant the songs of Zion, whose themes and melodies are molded by an extraordinary history.

by its own toil—given all that, the Jewish problem would be resolved. The Jews would again enter the family of nations as a natural entity, a normal nation.

In most ways they were right. If proof is needed, it is there, written on the faces of today's sabras. They are the ultimate testimony to the implementation of a mission, begun a hundred years ago, to restore in the ancestral home a sovereign freedom where Jews who so wish might, at last—and again—make their own independent decisions and live their own lives in accordance with their own needs, their own will, their own choice. This is the accomplishment of the Zionist enterprise.

It turns out, however, that the philosophies promulgated by many of the founders were not totally adequate. Normalization, it seems, is not always synonymous with normality. The former is a matter of self-image, the latter a matter of outside judgment. And herein lies the paradox: More than three decades after Israel's Declaration of Independence in its own homeland, there are some members of the family of nations which still do not relate to Israel as a natural and normal sovereign reality. They remain ambivalent toward it and there are even those who would wish to see it vanish, by force if need be, as experience has shown.

Undeniably, Israel remains something of an international curiosity, a normal enough country to most, but somehow different. To the children of Israel, this can at times be bewildering. For seen from their perspective, what, after all, is their land? It is a sliver of territory on the Mediterranean seaboard, a speck on the world map, a tiny member of the international community. Israel is so small that cartographers often cannot find space enough to print out its name without shedding some of it into the sea. And yet, the world's preoccupation with it is excessive and often obsessive. Something like sixty percent of the United Nations's annual agenda is traditionally devoted to the Jewish state, invariably to condemn it. International forums and power blocs rarely meet without having something to say about it. This tiny country seems to be forever news, accounting for a disproportionate amount of space in the world's press. It is no wonder that Israel's youngsters, as they grow older, sometimes feel that they are living under an international magnifying glass.

One can, of course, interpret all this in the context of realpolitik, of the insecurities of governments, even enlightened ones, engrossed in political and economic expedients caused by the dictates of oil blackmail. In a world where much is measured in terms of energy supply, rationality does not always prevail. This is sad, and more than being a reflection of Israel's failings, it is a commentary on the paranoia of oil-industry economies. How else can one explain the all too frequent habit that international forums have of seeking an Israeli cause for ills which have little or nothing to do with the Jewish state? True, the Israeli-Arab dispute has always been serious, but it is relatively minor compared to the really momentous conflicts that threaten mankind.

Perhaps there is an even deeper origin for this eccentricity, one that the Zionist founders failed to identify. They spoke of normality, but Jewish self-determination could not, by definition, have emerged through the normal processes of national self-determination as practiced by other peoples. Hence, Israel can never be understood by the usual criteria of international experience.

Israeli youngsters sometimes find this condition difficult to fathom—being the young inheritors of such an extraordinary history and a national heritage which challenges the conventional wisdoms.

227

Their country is so very old and so very new and the story of its modern sovereignty stands in such defiance of normal expectations. Never in history has a nation—exiled, scattered, harassed, and ultimately bled almost white—struggled to regain its national integrity and freedom and, in the end, a couple of thousand years later, done so. The children of Israel put a seal on an epitaph, twenty centuries long, whose final pages were written in the holocaust ashes of the graveless millions. They represent a totally unprecedented event. Israel fits no standard model or any neat cubbyhole of international reality, for the nature of its emergence simply has no parallel. Some governments find this hard to fathom.

Thirty-eight years after the children of Israel embarked on their Exodus from Egypt, and two years before they entered the Land of Israel, a certain heathen prophet, so the Bible records, articulated in astonishing terms the future destiny of the Jewish people. The prophet's name was Balaam and he said, "It is a people that shall dwell alone and shall not be reckoned among the nations." Whatever that means—and it is a mystery—one does not have to resort to mysticism to acknowledge that, for better or worse, the story of the Jewish people throughout the generations is characterized by a distinctiveness that stands quite alone—and the contemporary generation of the children of Israel is the inheritor of this experience. It is a burden, a responsibility, a privilege. Free and sovereign though Israel is, by the imperatives of its unique history and origin, it cannot be a state quite like others. Were it to be so, it would not be Jewish.

It is this, the distinctive Jewish self-perception—in some people self-inspired and in others hammered home by enemies—which has been the compulsion that built the edifice of statehood, turning marshland into meadow, desert into urban habitations, the tens of thousands into more than three million, and the constant warfare into the breakthrough to peace. This progression is the essential story of Israel.

True, the philosophers did not foresee all the awesome obstacles strewn along the path, and true, the founding fathers did not bequeath to the children of Israel the social utopia and the sovereign tranquillity which they had set out to found. But look at the youngsters and you see faces that reflect not another chapter in the annals of the Jewish people, but a new beginning altogether. For modern Israel is that—a new beginning. And its young inheritors will be the ones who will have to carry its remarkable story forward.